An Introduction to English Semantics and Pragmatics

Edinburgh Textbooks on the English Language

General Editor
Heinz Giegerich, Professor of English Linguistics, University of Edinburgh

TITLES IN THE SERIES INCLUDE:

Visit the Edinburgh Textbooks on the English Language website at
www.euppublishing.com/series/ETOTEL

An Introduction to English Semantics and Pragmatics

Second Edition

Patrick Griffiths
Revised by Chris Cummins

EDINBURGH
University Press

Edinburgh University Press is one of the leading university presses in the UK. We publish academic books and journals in our selected subject areas across the humanities and social sciences, combining cutting-edge scholarship with high editorial and production values to produce academic works of lasting importance. For more information visit our website: edinburghuniversitypress.com

First edition published 2006

Edinburgh University Press Ltd
The Tun – Holyrood Road
12(2f) Jackson's Entry
Edinburgh EH8 8PJ

Typeset in 10.5/12 Janson by
Servis Filmsetting Ltd, Stockport, Cheshire
and printed and bound in Great Britain by
CPI Group (UK) Ltd, Croydon CR0 4YY

A CIP record for this book is available from the British Library

ISBN 978 1 4744 1281 0 (hardback)
ISBN 978 1 4744 1283 4 (paperback)
ISBN 978 1 4744 1282 7 (webready PDF)
ISBN 978 1 4744 1284 1 (epub)

Contents

List of figures and tables

Figures

Tables

Preface to the first edition

I chose Edinburgh University for postgraduate studies because I wanted to learn semantics from John Lyons, one of whose books I had read. It turned out that he was not teaching semantics the year that I took the taught graduate course, but there were eventually seminars of his that I could attend, and I read more of his work. His influence can be traced in this book. It was Martin Atkinson, a fellow research assistant on an Edinburgh University Linguistics Department project, who first explained to me how the study of meaning can be split between semantics and pragmatics. Semantics is concerned with the resources (vocabulary and a system for calculating phrase-, clause- and sentence-meanings) provided by a language, and pragmatics is concerned with how those resources are put to use in communication. My grasp got firmer when I began to teach semantics and pragmatics myself at York University (UK), and later at the University of the South Pacific, York St John and Beppu University (Japan). Finding examples that communicate a point but which cannot easily be dismissed or misunderstood by students is a valuable discipline, especially when one tries to figure out, in relation to particular theoretical notions, what it takes to be a good example.

I am grateful that Heinz Giegerich, general editor of this series, came up with the idea of introductory textbooks offering compact descriptions of English unobtrusively grounded in defensible theory – it is an approach congenial to my ways of teaching and learning. My contribution to the series aims to present a reasonably detailed first look at the main features of the meaning system of English and the pragmatics of using that system. I owe thanks to Anthony Warner for encouraging me to write the book. In lunchtime conversations that I used to have with him at York University, he several times straightened out muddled ideas of mine regarding meaning. Beppu University provided me with an environment conducive to writing. Professor Kenji Ueda, Head of the English Language and Literature Department, encouraged me and also kindly authorised the purchase of some of the books that I needed to consult.

Pragmatics deals with inferences that listeners and readers make, or that – when speaking or writing – they invite others to make. These inferences are often conscious, so pragmatics tends to be easier to understand than semantics, because the latter is about abstract potential meanings that are often best described by means of notations drawn from logic and set theory. Linguistic meaning cannot usefully be studied by someone who knows only about pragmatics, however. A view widely shared among linguists is that semantics and pragmatics are essential components that work together in a full description of meaning. In this book I attempt to integrate semantics with pragmatics. The pragmatics is Gricean, supplemented by Austin–Searle speech acts, and making use in a couple of places of ideas from Relevance Theory.

Theoretical concepts and technical terms are introduced to the extent needed for making essential points in the description of meaning in English. Though the book is a self-standing introduction to English semantics and pragmatics, I hope that readers will be interested enough to want to learn more. For any who have the opportunity to do additional reading, the terminology introduced here should suffice for them to make headway with a range of intermediate-level books about semantics and pragmatics. At the end of each chapter there is a section of recommendations for further reading. Bold printed items in the index point to places in the text where technical terms are explained – not just when they first come up, but also to any subsequent elaborations.

Sarah Edwards, Commissioning Editor at Edinburgh University Press, provided clear guidance and responded efficiently to queries. She earned even greater gratitude from me for her forbearance in the face of my repeated failures to deliver chapters on time. Norman Macleod, as a member of the Editorial Board, scrutinised first drafts of all the chapters and read a revised version of the whole book too. Norman made very concise suggestions for improvements and alerted me to a number of subtleties in English meaning and usage. Heinz Giegerich kindly read a near-final version of the whole text. I thank James Dale, the Managing Desk Editor, and Sarah Burnett, the Copy Editor, for quality control on the text. Near the end, Andrew Merrison, doing it simply as a favour for a fellow linguist, read the book and passed on a list of inconsistencies, mistypings and questionable punctuations, many of which have now been eliminated.

Janet Griffiths, my spouse, supported me throughout and was the person most available for verification (or a headshake) of my intuitions about meaning. She checked drafts of several of the chapters and diagnosed confusing wording in quite a few places. I thank her with all my heart. Jane Griffiths visited around the time that I finished a second version of the chapter on figurative language. She read it and offered comments that I appreciated. Thanks, Jane.

Preface to the second edition

I was honoured to be asked to revise this textbook. In doing so, I have attempted to bring the contents up to date while continuing to respect and retain the clarity and readability of the original text.

In the first edition, Patrick Griffiths drew an analogy with 'slow food' and modestly expressed a regret that not all of the book was "composed in a measured and reflective way". This did not strike me when reading his work. However, pursuing the culinary analogy, one advantage that I do have in preparing this second edition is that generations of readers have sampled the original and a few have offered suggestions as to how to tweak the recipe. As the sous-chef I take the blame for any failings in the result. Nevertheless, I should like to thank Heinz Giegerich and Ronnie Cann for their useful feedback on an initial draft.

1 Studying meaning

Overview

This book is about how the English language allows people to convey meanings. As the title suggests, semantics and pragmatics are the two main branches of the linguistic study of meaning. **Semantics** is the study of the relationship between units of language and their meaning. **Pragmatics** is concerned with how we use language in communication, and therefore involves the interaction of semantic knowledge with our knowledge of the world, including such things as the contexts in which we use language.

Explanations of terms
Numbers in **bold print** in the index point to the pages where technical terms, such as **semantics** and **pragmatics** in the paragraph above, are explained.

To illustrate some of the differences between semantics and pragmatics, let's consider example (1.1).

(1.1)   Hold out your arm. That's it.

Language enables us to communicate about the world outside of language. There are conventional links between expressions in the English language and aspects of the world (real or imagined) that language users talk and write about: things, activities, and so on. We sometimes use the word **denote** to describe these links. *Hold out* denotes an action; *arm* denotes a part of a person; *your arm* denotes the arm of the person being addressed; and so on. An **expression** is any meaningful language unit or sequence of meaningful units, such as a sentence, a clause, a phrase, a word or a meaningful part of a word (such as the *s* of *cats*,

1

which denotes plurality, but not the *s* of *is*, which doesn't have a separate meaning).

That's it is an expression that can mean several things, including something like 'OK' and something like 'There is no more to say'. But what do the expressions *that* and *it* separately denote? *That* denotes something that is assumed to be obvious to the addressee: it could be a physical object, or an abstract concept, or even an action or event such as the act of holding out an arm. *It* usually denotes something that has recently been spoken about: this too could be an object or an action or event. Without knowing the context in which (1.1) occurred, its meaning cannot be explained in much more detail than this.

In fact, (1.1) is a quotation from the first of J. K. Rowling's Harry Potter novels.[1] It is spoken by Mr Ollivander, a supplier of fine wands, and occurs just after he has taken out a tape-measure and asked Harry 'Which is your wand arm?' This context makes it highly likely that *your arm* in (1.1) denotes Harry's wand arm. Immediately after (1.1), Mr Ollivander begins to measure Harry for a wand. This helps us understand that Harry complied with the request to hold out his arm, and that "That's it" was said to acknowledge that he had done so. In fact, we might be able to go further: we could say that *that* denotes the action Harry performed, *it* denotes the previous specification of what he was asked to do, and *'s* (a form of *is*) indicates that these two things match: he had done what he was asked to do. But whether the expression is really analysable in this way, or whether it functions just as a fixed expression, isn't easy to determine.

What this example illustrates is that there is an interplay between semantics and pragmatics. Semantics provides a set of possible meanings, and pragmatics is concerned with the choice among the semantic possibilities. Language users can take account of context, and use their general knowledge about how the world works, in order to build interpretations on this semantic foundation.

This view fits with a way of thinking about communication that was pioneered by the philosopher H. P. Grice in the mid-twentieth century (see Grice 1989 for a collection of relevant work) and which has been highly influential within linguistics. According to this view, human communication is not like merely pressing buttons on a remote control, or transmitting data through a telecom network. Rather, it requires active collaboration on the part of the **addressee** or **hearer** (the person the message is directed to), such as the reader of (1.1) in the context of its book, or Harry Potter hearing the utterance in the context of the story. The addressee's task is to try to guess what the **speaker** intends to convey, and the message has been communicated when (and only when) the speaker's intention has been recognised. (By convention, I'll refer to the 'speaker' and the 'hearer' whether we're actually talking about speech or written communication.) The speaker's task is to judge what needs to be said (or written) in order for this process to work: that is, so that it's possible for the hearer to recognise their intention.

This view has several important consequences:

- The same string of words can convey different messages, because – depending on the context – there will be different clues to help the hearer recognise the speaker's intention.
- Similarly, different strings of words can be used to convey the same message, because there are different possible ways for the speaker to give clues to their intention.
- Sometimes a great deal can be communicated with very few words, because of the active participation of the hearer in recovering the speaker's meaning.
- Mistakes are possible. In face-to-face interactions the speaker can monitor the listeners' reactions to judge whether or not their communication has been successful, and can say more in order to allay misunderstandings and further guide the hearer towards what is intended. This is still possible, but to a more limited extent, in live telephone conversations, less still in email exchanges, and even less in books (although writers may eventually discover something about how what they wrote has been understood or misunderstood).

The rest of this chapter introduces other concepts that are important to the study of linguistic meaning, and indicates which later chapters develop them further. It will introduce a few more technical terms, but (hopefully) just enough to give you a reasonable initial grasp on semantics and pragmatics and set you up for reading introductory books in this area.

Competent users of a language generally use it without giving much thought to the details of what is going on. Linguists in general operate on the assumption that there are interesting things to discover in those details. This can appear a little obsessive, and the discussion of (1.1) might have been heading in that direction, but the general project of linguistics involves trying to bring all this unconscious knowledge to conscious awareness. Close inspection of bits of language and instances of usage – even quite ordinary ones – can sometimes give us fascinating insights into how they really work.

1.1 Sentences and utterances

An important distinction for our purposes will be that between sentences and utterances. Utterances are the things that have meaning in our immediate experience as language users. (1.2) presents three examples.

(1.2) a. "Sure." (Something I said in a colleague's office this afternoon.)

  b. "By the departments." (Said by the convenor of a meeting today.)

  c. "I can't stand myself." (Something I recall a friend saying many years ago.)

Utterances are the raw data for our linguistic analysis. Each utterance is unique, having been produced by a particular speaker in a particular situation. (Just as we use the term "speaker" to mean the sender of a particular message, whether that's in speech or writing, we use the term "utterance" to refer to parts of that message, regardless of whether or not it is literally "uttered".) Utterances can never precisely be repeated because they are tied to the speaker and the context. If I say "Sure" again, in a different context to the utterance of (1.2a), that is a different utterance (and will convey a different meaning). Even when someone "says the same thing twice", as in the case of someone who repeats themselves (or repeats what someone else has said), the two utterances differ, because the context has changed. Although no one keeps a record of every utterance, in principle they are all distinguishable.

Notation
When it matters, I use " " double quotes for utterances, ' ' single quotes for meanings, and *italics* for sentences and words being considered in the abstract. I also use single quotes when quoting other authors, and double quotes as "scare quotes" around expressions that are not strictly accurate but potentially useful approximations.

The abstract linguistic object on which an utterance is based is a **sentence**. For instance, (1.2b) was apparently based on the sentence *The number of students is estimated by the departments*, as it was uttered in answer to a question "How is the number of students estimated?" The cases of repetition discussed above are often cases where two or more utterances are based on the same sentence.

Utterances are interpreted in context. The context of (1.2c) made it reasonably clear that the intended meaning was that the speaker was not personally able to stand for election to a committee post, and that *myself* was to be understood as emphasising the subject of the sentence, rather than as an object for the transitive verb *stand* meaning 'to tolerate' (in which case the utterance would convey that the speaker disliked himself). You might expect that the speaker's delivery would indicate which of these two meanings was intended, and that for the intended meaning there would be an intonational break before *myself*, which in transcribing the sentence could be marked with a comma. In practice, things are not always so clear-cut and ambiguities can easily arise as to which sentence underlies a given utterance. In any case, intonation does not remove the need to consider context: we tend to use context to check that we have understood the intonation correctly, and to use intonation as a clue to which contextual information to use.

1.2 Types of meaning

Speaker meaning is the meaning that the speaker intends to convey by means of an utterance. This is something that hearers are continually having to make informed guesses about. The hearer's response, either in words or actions, can give an indication of how they have interpreted the utterance, and this interpretation can be confirmed or corrected by the speaker (or other hearers). However, sometimes the speaker may not be able to convey their meaning any better than they have already done by producing the utterance.

Speaker meanings are the communicative goals of the speakers and the interpretational targets for the hearers. They are private: speakers may not want to admit overtly that they intended to convey certain meanings. Utterances, however, are publicly observable – they are witnessed by the hearer and may be recorded. We cannot be sure that speaker meaning always matches the hearer's interpretation, so there is something of a dilemma over what to regard as the meaning of an utterance. Is it the speaker's meaning or the interpretation arrived at by the hearer(s)? We cannot know precisely what either of those is, in a given instance. However, as language users, we gain experience as both speakers and hearers, and develop intuitions about the meaning an utterance is likely to carry in a given context. So **utterance meaning** is a necessary fiction that linguists doing semantics and pragmatics have to work with. It is the meaning that an utterance would likely be understood as conveying when interpreted by people who know the language, are aware of the context, and have whatever background knowledge could reasonably be assumed by the speaker.

Because utterances are instances of sentences in use, an important first step towards understanding utterance meaning is understanding **sentence meaning**. I'll take this to be the meaning that people familiar with the language can agree on for sentences considered in isolation.

Ordinary language users have readily accessible intuitions about sentences. For instance, people proficient in English can easily recognise that the sentence in (1.3a) has two meanings, as shown in (1.3b) and (1.3c) – that is, it is **ambiguous**.

(1.3)   a.   *He is a conductor.*
      b.   'He checks tickets on public transport'
      c.   'He regulates the performance of a musical group'

Language users' access to the meanings of words is less direct. We can think of the meaning of a word as the contribution it makes to the meanings of sentences in which it appears. Of course, people know the meanings of words in their language in the sense that they know how to use the words, but this knowledge is not immediately available in the form of reliable intuitions. Speakers of English might be willing to agree that *strong* means the same as *powerful*, or that *finish* means the same as *stop*: but these judgements would be at least partly wrong, as shown when we compare (1.4a) with (1.4b), and (1.4c) with (1.4d).

(1.4)   a.   Mavis stopped writing the assignment yesterday, but she hasn't finished writing it yet.
      b.   *Mavis finished writing the assignment yesterday, but she hasn't stopped writing it yet.
      c.   This cardboard box is strong.
      d.   ?This cardboard box is powerful.

Notation

Asterisks, like the one at the beginning of (1.4b), are used in semantics to indicate that an example is seriously problematic as far as meaning goes – in this case, the sentence is a contradiction. Question marks, like the one at the beginning of (1.4d), are used to signal oddness of meaning to a less serious extent.

From the above examples, we might conclude that *finishing* is a special kind of *stopping*, specifically 'stopping after the goal has been reached', and that *strong* can mean either 'durable' or 'powerful' (among other possibilities), only one of which is applicable to cardboard boxes.

1.2.1 Denotation, sense, reference and deixis

Near the beginning of this chapter, expressions in a language – sentences, words, and so forth – were said to denote aspects of the world. The **denotation** of an expression is whatever it denotes. For many words, their denotation is a large class of things: the noun *thing* itself would be an extreme example. If expressions did not have denotations, languages would not be of much use: it is the fact that they allow us to communicate about the world that makes them so indispensable.

Because languages have useful links to the world, it is tempting to think that the meaning of an expression is simply its denotation. You would certainly stand a chance of explaining the meaning of a word such as *arm* to someone who didn't know it by saying that word as you pointed to their arms or waved your own. In early childhood, our first words are probably learnt through just such a process of live demonstration and pointing, known as **ostension**. However, this is not plausible as a general explanation of how meaning is acquired, for several reasons including the following:

* It ignores the fact that, after early childhood, we usually use language rather than ostension to explain the meanings of words (*"Flee* means 'escape by running away'"), and when we do use ostension we often explain it further with accompanying utterances. For instance, if we just said *beige* while pointing to a piece of toffee, it would be unclear whether we meant that *beige* was another word for toffee, or food in general, or 'sticky', or the colour of the toffee. We would be more likely to explain the meaning by pointing at the toffee and saying *"Beige* is this colour".
* There are all kinds of abstract, non-existent and relational denotations that cannot conveniently be explained by ostension: consider *memory, absence, yeti* or *instead of.*

There are two general solutions which are compatible but which address the problem in different ways. The approach taken in **formal semantics** (so called because it uses systems of formal logic to set out descriptions of meaning, and theories of how the meanings of expressions relate to the meanings of their parts; see Lappin 2001) accords importance to differences between kinds of denotation. Thus, count nouns, such as *tree,* may be said to denote sets of things; mass nouns, like *honey*, denote substances; singular names denote individuals; property words, like *purple*, denote sets of things (the things that have the property in question); spatial relation words, like *in*, denote pairs of things that are linked by that spatial relation; simple sentences such as *Amsterdam is in Holland* denote facts or falsehoods; and so on. What is of interest is the fact that the denotation is what it is – an individual, or a set of things, or a set of pairs of things, and so on.

Another approach takes **sense** to be the central concept: that is, those aspects of the meaning of an expression that give it the denotation it has. Differences in sense therefore make for differences in denotation. Example (1.3), for instance, illustrated two senses of *conductor*, and a third sense of this word concerns a substance that transmits electricity, heat, light or sound. I believe this approach offers a helpful way into the linguistic study of meaning, and it will be presented in this book in a version that forms a reasonable foundation for anyone who later chooses to learn formal semantics.

There are different ways in which we might try to write down "recipes" for the denotations of words. One way of doing this is in terms of **sense relations**, which are semantic relationships between the senses of expressions.[2] This is the scheme that is going to be used in this book. It harmonises well with the observation that we commonly use language to explain meanings. (1.5) gives some examples of the kind of thing we know as a consequence of understanding English sense relations: notice that they amount to (partial) explanations of meanings.

(1.5)   an *arm* is a *limb*
         an *arm* is an *upper limb*
         a *leg* is a *limb*
         a *leg* is a *lower limb*
         a *person* has an *arm*
         an *arm* has a *hand* and a *wrist* and an *elbow*
         extend is a synonym of *hold out*
         pursue is the converse of *flee*

Sense relations between words, and some phrases, will be further explained and illustrated in the following chapter. The reason that sense relations bear upon denotation is that, with words interconnected by well-defined sense relations, a person who knows the denotations of some words can develop an understanding of some of the meanings (senses) in the rest of the system.

Reference is what speakers do when they use expressions to pick out particular entities for their audience: people ("my sister"), things ("the Parthenon Marbles"), times ("October 21, 2015"), places ("that corner"), events ("her party"), etc. Examples of **referring expressions** – expressions that pick out referents – are given in parentheses. The actual entities being referred to are called the **referents** of the referring expressions. Reference has to be performed and interpreted with regard to context. Consider (1.6), where the speaker intends to use *Edinburg* to refer to the city of that name in Indiana.

(1.6)   "We drove to Edinburg today."

The speaker of (1.6) would have to be sure that the hearer knows that they are in Indiana if the utterance is not to be misunderstood as refer-ring to the Edinburg in Illinois, or the one in Texas, or even Edinburgh in Scotland.

When using the pronoun "we", the speaker of (1.6) refers to herself or himself plus (usually) at least one other person. Similarly, "today" refers to the day on which the utterance was made. If (1.6) occurs as part of an email, it will probably be trivial to determine when it was sent, and therefore what "today" refers to; and given sufficient context, it will probably also be possible to work out which set of people "we" refers to. On the other hand, if (1.6) is originally part of a letter which is then torn up, and a stranger finds a scrap of paper with just (1.6) written on it, they will not be able to discern who the travellers were, which Edinburg they drove to, or when they did so.

Similarly, a course bulletin board once carried a notice saying (1.7).

(1.7)   "The first tutorial will be held next week."

The notice was posted in week 1 of the academic year, but not dated, and the tutor forgot to take it down. Some students read it in week 2 and failed to attend the week 2 tutorial because they interpreted "next week" to mean "week 3".

Deictic expressions (cases of **deixis**) are words, phrases and features of grammar that have to be interpreted in relation to the situation in which they are uttered, such as *me* ("the speaker of this utterance"), *here* ("the place where the speaker is") or *next week* ("the week after the time of utterance").

Deixis is pervasive in language, presumably because speaking with reference to the here and now is a good way to describe times, places, etc. There are different kinds of deixis, relating to:

- time: *now, soon, recently, ago, tomorrow, next week* . . .
- place: *here, there, two kilometres away, that side, this way, come, bring, upstairs* . . .

- persons and entities: *she, her, hers, he, him, his, they, it, this, that . . .*
- discourse itself: *this sentence, the next paragraph, that's what she said, this is true . . .*

Our semantic knowledge of the meanings of deictic expressions guides us as to how we should interpret them in context. As always, where context is concerned, these interpretations will be guesses rather than certainties: when you infer that the speaker is using *this* to refer to an object at which he seems to be pointing, you could be wrong – perhaps he is referring to the ring on his index finger.

Much of language is in some sense deictic: tense, which will be discussed in Chapter 6, is deictic. More will also be said about reference in many of the following chapters, but especially Chapter 10.

1.3 Semantics vs pragmatics

As we've seen, the essential difference between sentences and utterances is that sentences are abstract, and not tied to contexts, whereas utterances are identified by their contexts. This is also the main way of distinguishing between semantics and pragmatics. If you are dealing with meaning and there is no context to consider, then you are doing semantics, but if there is a context to consider, then you are engaged in pragmatics. **Pragmatics** is the study of utterance meaning. **Semantics** is the study of sentence meaning and word meaning.

To illustrate this, consider how we might interpret (1.8).

(1.8)   The next bus goes to Cramond.

The **literal meaning** of a sentence is just based on the semantic information that you have from your knowledge of the language. Someone who knows English can explain various aspects of the meaning of (1.8): for instance, that it means that a bus goes to Cramond, and that the bus that does so is in some sense the 'next bus'. Moreover, *goes* can be understood in two ways – as making a prediction about what the next bus will do, or stating a generalisation about where that bus habitually goes. These meanings are available without wondering who might say or write the words, when or where: no consideration of context is involved. Hence, their study falls within the domain of semantics.

In context, we can arrive at a richer understanding of the meaning of (1.8) by considering **implicature**: that is, what is hinted at by an utterance in its particular context. Suppose that Ann steps onto a bus and asks the driver whether this bus goes to Cramond, and the driver replies by uttering (1.8). Assuming that the driver is being cooperative, we can interpret (1.8) as conveying an answer of "no" to Ann's question. This is an inference that is derived by trying to understand, in the light of contextual and background information, the point of a speaker producing the utterance that he or she did. We cannot ignore the literal meaning of (1.8) in deriving this implicature – literal meaning is the foundation for implicature – but nor can we claim that (1.8) generally means 'no'. For this reason, the study of implicature falls within the domain of pragmatics.

However, there are additional forms of meaning whose status with regard to the semantics–pragmatics division is not clear. An **explicature** is a basic interpretation of an utterance, using contextual information and world knowledge to work out what is being referred to and how to understand ambiguous expressions. In the case of (1.8), the question of which bus is the "next bus" is dependent on the time at which the sentence is uttered. This is generally true for the establishment of reference, the resolution of deictic expressions, and so on. We might argue that the explicature is part of pragmatics because it is context-dependent, or that the explicature is part of semantics because it is essential to the meaning of the utterance in a way that implicature is not. I will try to avoid that theoretical debate here, but the notion of explicature will be appealed to in the discussion of figurative language in Chapter 9.

1.3.1 A first outline of semantics

Semantics, the study of word meaning and sentence meaning abstracted away from contexts of use, is primarily a descriptive subject. It is an attempt to describe and understand the nature of the knowledge about meaning in a language that people have as a consequence of knowing that language. It is not a prescriptive enterprise with an interest in advising or pressuring speakers into abandoning some meanings and adopting others (though prescriptivists can certainly benefit from studying the semantics of a language that they want to lay down rules about). A related point is that one can know a language perfectly well without knowing its history. While it may be fascinating to understand how different meanings are associated with forms which share historical origins – *arms, armour, army, armada, armadillo*, etc. – this kind of knowledge is not essential for using present-day English, so it is not covered in this book. Nor does this book focus on semantic and pragmatic change, although that may be of great interest to historical linguistics (and we will occasionally discuss processes that may also be implicated in historical change).

The process of giving a semantic description of language knowledge is also different from the encyclopedia-writer's task of cataloguing general knowledge. The words *tangerine* and *clementine* illustrate a distinction that may not be part of our knowledge of English: although an expert will be able to tell these apart, most users of English will not. As we will see, there are many more abstract kinds of semantic knowledge in play, some of which are crucial to the successful use of language.

1.3.2 A first outline of pragmatics

Pragmatics is concerned with characterising how we go beyond what was literally said, both in terms of what additional content is conveyed and in terms of how that takes place. A crucial basis for making pragmatic inferences is the contrast between what might have been uttered and what actually was uttered. Example (1.9) is a short headed section from a flyer about a restaurant.

(1.9)   "Alcohol & Smoking. You are welcome to bring your own alcohol provided you are buying a meal. There is no charge for doing so."

The leaflet then switches to another topic, inviting us to infer that no provision is made for smoking: however, we cannot be certain about this. Perhaps the restaurateurs intended to mention some provision for smoking, but neglected to do so. Nevertheless, the absence of such a reference – under the relevant heading – could certainly be interpreted as a pointedly negative hint to smokers. This implicature is clearly an elaboration that goes far beyond the literal meaning of what appears in the leaflet.

A further and more obvious pragmatic enrichment is the implicature that you cannot bring alcohol if you are not buying a meal. It is not clear that this follows from the literal meaning of (1.9): we could say that (1.9) expresses permission to bring alcohol if you are buying a meal, but neither permits nor forbids the bringing of alcohol for patrons who are not buying a meal. In this case, we could naturally interpret the fact that "provided you are buying a meal" is mentioned at all to signal that this is a necessary condition for bringing alcohol. In this case, the implicature is so natural that we might mistake it for part of the literal meaning, but it does seem to depend on reasoning about possible alternative utterances.

Another widely available pragmatic inference, often called a **scalar implicature**, arises when words can be ordered on a semantic scale, as for example the value judgements *excellent* > *good* > *OK*.

(1.10) A: "What was the accommodation like at the camp?"
B: "It was OK."

Speaker A can draw an inference from B's response, because if the accommodation had been better than merely OK, B could have used the word *good* or indeed *excellent* to describe it. As B does not do so, A can infer that the accommodation was no better than satisfactory. Again, this is to some extent dependent on contextual factors: we might expect that B is speaking in an unenthusiastic tone of voice. By contrast, if B produces the same utterance with a surprised intonation, this inference may be less readily available: B's utterance might then be interpreted as meaning something like 'contrary to expectations, it was acceptable, and maybe even better than that'.

Pragmatic inferences of this kind occur all the time in communication: even though they are merely informed guesses, they are crucial to the smooth functioning of much of our communication. As informed guesses, it is one of their defining features that they can be cancelled. In (1.10), B could continue "In fact, it was good" without being self-contradictory, because what is 'good' in this case is also 'OK'. Pragmatics is the focus of the later chapters of this book, but will also figure in sections of most of the other chapters.

Summary

Hearers (including readers) have the task of guessing what speakers (including writers) intend to communicate when they produce utterances. If the guess is correct, the speaker has succeeded in conveying the meaning. Pragmatics is about how we interpret utterances – and produce interpretable utterances – taking account of context and background knowledge. Semantics is the study of the context-independent knowledge that users of a language have about the meanings of expressions, such as words and sentences. Crucially, expressions of language relate to the world outside of language. In this book, we will explore this idea through the notion of sense and of the meaning relations that hold within a language, in ways that should become clearer in later chapters.

Exercises

1. Here are two sets of words: {*arrive, be at/in, leave*} and {*learn, know, forget*}. There is a similarity between these two sets, in how the words relate to one another. Can you see it? Here is a start: someone who is not at a place gets to be there by arriving; what if the person then

leaves? Once you have found the similarities between the two sets, answer this follow-up question: was this a semantic or a pragmatic task?

2. A student says to the tutor "How did I do in the exam?" and the tutor replies "You didn't fail." What the tutor opted to say allows the student to guess at the sort of grade achieved. Do you think the grade was high or low? How confident are you about this? Briefly justify your answer. In doing this, were you doing semantics or pragmatics?

3. *Pick the right lock* is an ambiguous sentence. State at least two meanings it can have. How many different propositions could be involved?

4. A common myth about the word *kangaroo* is that it comes from an Australian language (specifically Guugu Yimithirr) phrase meaning 'I don't understand you', supposedly because explorers in the eighteenth century pointed to a kangaroo and asked what it was, and a local replied *kangaroo*. What does this story tell us about the limits of ostension? And how would we disprove the claim that this is what *kangaroo* originally meant?

5. An old joke concerns someone reading a sign saying *Dogs must be carried on this escalator* and having to wait ages for a dog to appear so that they could use the escalator. If that sign really caused people any problems, how could you add a deictic term to it and thus resolve the ambiguity?

Recommendations for reading

Textbooks offering more detail on semantics include Saeed (2015) and Kearns (2011), the latter offering a particularly good introduction to formal semantics. Elbourne (2011) provides a concise introduction into the important theoretical and philosophical questions for semantics. Cruse (2011) offers many interesting insights into word meanings. On the pragmatic side, Huang (2006) is a good introduction, and Levinson (1983) remains insightful.

Notes

1. J. K. Rowling (1997), *Harry Potter and the Philosopher's Stone*, London: Bloomsbury, p. 94.
2. This approach was given impetus in the 1960s–80s by the semanticist Sir John Lyons (see for instance Lyons 1977).

2 Sense relations

Overview

As mentioned in Chapter 1, we generally come to know the meanings of our first few words, in early childhood, through close encounters with the world, painstakingly mediated by our caregivers. But once we have a start in a language, we learn the meanings of most other words through language itself. This might involve having the meanings deliberately explained to us ("*Tiny* means 'very small'") or drawing inferences about the meanings based on our knowledge of language (for instance, inferring from the title of Gerald Durrell's book *My Family and Other Animals* that there is a view according to which people can be classified as a type of animal).

The focus of this book is the systematic description of meaning relationships within a language, between the senses of expressions (words and phrases). The ultimate aim is to produce an economical and insightful statement of the knowledge about linguistic meaning that a competent language user possesses. But before we can describe some of these sense relations in more detail, we will need some technical preliminaries, which I'll introduce in the following subsection.

2.1 Propositions and entailment

We need to account for sentence meaning in order to develop explanations of utterance meaning, because utterances are sentences put to use. The number of sentences in a human language is potentially infinite, so we cannot elucidate the meanings of sentences simply by writing them all down and providing each with an interpretation (either when we are conducting linguistic analysis, or when we are acquiring our language). We have to generalise in order to try to discover the principles of sentence meaning.

One important observation in this regard is that different sentences can carry the same meaning, as in (2.1a–c).

(2.1) a. Sharks hunt seals.
       b. Seals are hunted by sharks.
       c. Seals are prey to sharks.

Proposition is a term for the kind of core sentence meaning that remains the same between (2.1a–c). Propositions in this sense are abstract, and are not tied to particular words or sentences. The only feature that all propositions have is that they are, in principle, either true or false. That is not to say that the speaker or hearer (or anyone else) needs to know whether the proposition is actually true or false, as far as the real world is concerned: it's just to say that a proposition must in principle either be true or false.

The sentences in (2.1) are declaratives, the sentence pattern on which **statements** (utterances that explicitly convey factual information) are based. It is easy to see that they express propositions, because it is possible to affirm or deny or query the truth of these propositions ("Yes, that's true", "No, that's a lie", "Is that really true?") This kind of response is not appropriate to utterances such as (2.2a–b), which are based on other sentence patterns.

(2.2) a. What's your name?
       b. Please help me.

Although these utterances, and many others like them, do not express propositions, we could analyse them as involving propositions. We could think of (2.2a) as carrying a proposition of the form 'the hearer's name is ___', and cooperative hearers will supply their name to fill the gap. Similarly, we could say that (2.2b) presents a proposition 'the hearer will help the speaker' in such a way as to indicate that the speaker wants that proposition to be made true. Alternatively, and perhaps more usefully, we can describe utterances of this kind in terms of the social actions that speakers are trying to perform when they produce the utterances, as we shall see in Chapter 11 when discussing speech acts.

An important relation that holds between propositions is **entailment**, which we can write as ⇒.[1] We say that one proposition entails another (p ⇒ q, "p entails q") if the first proposition being true guarantees that the second is also true. Entailment is also called "logical consequence" and is one of the most fundamental concepts in logic: arguments are logically valid if and only if the starting points (premises) entail the conclusions. Although entailment holds between propositions, we can

think of it holding between sentences if we make sure that we are considering each sentence with just one of its meanings.

The examples in (2.3) illustrate some of these points.

(2.3)   a.   Moira has arrived in Edinburgh.
        b.   Moira is in Edinburgh.
        c.   Moira has arrived in Edinburgh ⇒ Moira is in Edinburgh
        d.   *Moira has arrived in Edinburgh and she is not in Edinburgh.

When (2.3a) is true we can be sure that (2.3b) is also true (provided that
we are talking about the same Moira and the same Edinburgh). That
means that the entailment shown in (2.3c) holds. Another way of stating
this is that (2.3d) is a contradiction: given that (2.3a) entails (2.3b), we
cannot sensibly affirm (2.3a) and the negation of (2.3b) at the same time.
To put this in more general terms, if we have propositions p and q such
that p ⇒ q, we know that the complex proposition "p & not-q" is necessarily false.

(2.3a) has other entailments, as shown in (2.4).

(2.4)   a.   Moira has arrived in Edinburgh ⇒ Moira is not in
             Birmingham
        b.   Moira has arrived in Edinburgh ⇒ Moira went to Edinburgh

The word *arrived* is an important contributor to (2.3a) having the
entailments shown. If *lived* or *been* were substituted for *arrived*, the
entailments would be different. If someone were to ask what *arrive*
meant, a sentence like (2.3a) could be given as an example, explaining
that it means that Moira journeyed from somewhere else and is now in
Edinburgh. However, the entailments from a sentence depend not only
upon the words in the sentence but also upon their grammatical organisation. For instance, the grammatical construction with *has*, sometimes
called the present perfect construction, is crucial to the entailment in
(2.3c); see Chapter 6 for further discussion.

If (2.3a) is understood and accepted as true, then none of its
entailments need to be put into words. They follow automatically,
and can be inferred from (2.3a) by the hearer. It is obviously crucial to
successful language use for speakers to make sure that the sentences that
they utter have the correct entailments. We can think of the **sense** of a
word in terms of the particular entailment possibilities that sentences
get as a result of containing that word: whichever aspects of the word's
meaning that are responsible for the sentences having those entailments
are its sense.

2.1.1 Meaning postulates

Meaning postulates were developed by the philosopher Rudolf Carnap (1891–1970) as a way of integrating the entailment information that comes from word meanings into logical systems. Although the technicalities of this approach aren't crucial for this book, a short account of it should help you appreciate some of the wider significance of semantic description.

First, we need to distinguish between inferences that depend solely on structure and inferences that also depend upon the meanings of particular words.

(2.5)   Rupert is a friend of mine
                and if he is a friend of mine then I am willing to lend him
                my bicycle.
                        Therefore I am willing to lend Rupert my bicycle.

The inference at the end of (2.5) – after the word *therefore* – depends entirely on the structure of that discourse. The reasoning is valid simply because it fits a particular pattern that always yields true conclusions if the premises (initial statements) are true. The pattern is set out in (2.6).

(2.6)   p
                & (if p then q)
                        Therefore q

When both of the premises (the first two lines) are true, the conclusion must also be true. To emphasise that it is the structure of the discourse that ensures validity here, rather than the individual words or the particular ideas being spoken about, (2.7) presents another instance of the same pattern.

(2.7)   We are sailing towards the Arctic
                and if we are sailing towards the Arctic then we are
                heading northwards.
                        Therefore we are heading northwards.

By contrast, (2.8) presents an inference that depends crucially upon the meanings of particular words.

(2.8)   The A380 is bigger than a B747.
                Therefore a B747 is smaller than the A380.

This argument is accepted as valid by people who know English (even if they do not recognise that the sentence is about two kinds of aircraft). However, its validity does not follow from the structure of the discourse.

'p therefore q' is not generally a valid line of reasoning, as shown by the obvious invalidity of (2.9).

(2.9)   Rupert is a friend of mine.
                Therefore we are heading northwards.

Some additional ingredient is needed in order to explain why the reasoning in (2.8) makes sense, and that ingredient is provided by a meaning postulate. The particular meaning postulate required in this case has to represent a linguistic fact about English – when one thing X is *bigger* than another thing Y, then Y is *smaller* than X.

The particular sense relation exhibited by *bigger* and *smaller* will be discussed in Section 2.4. The important thing to bear in mind is that that relation, along with the other sense relations discussed in this chapter, can be represented within systems of formal logic. (Cann 1993: 218–24 offers an account that explicitly accommodates sense relations, although that presentation assumes familiarity with symbolic logic.)

2.2 Compositionality

Given the potentially infinite supply of distinct sentences in a language, semanticists aim to develop a **compositional** theory of meaning. The **principle of compositionality** is the idea that the meaning of a complex expression is determined by the meanings of its parts and how those parts are put together. The idea that human language is compositional in this sense has a very long history; among other things, it offers a partial explanation of how we can comprehend the meanings of infinitely many different potential sentences, just by knowing the meanings of finitely many different sentence parts (and their combining rules). The meaningful parts of a sentence are clauses, phrases and words, and the meaningful parts of words are **morphemes**.

To draw a simple analogy with arithmetic, several things affect the result of an arithmetical operation: the numbers that are involved, the operations, and (where there are multiple operations) the order in which the operations take place, as shown in (2.10).

(2.10)   a. $3 + 2 = 5$ but $3 + 4 = 7$
             b. $3 + 2 = 5$ but $3 \times 2 = 6$
             c. $3 \times (2 + 4) = 18$ but $(3 \times 2) + 4 = 10$

The examples in (2.11) show something similar to what we see in (2.10c). Here our operations are not addition and multiplication, but negation (or reversal) performed by the prefix *un-* and the formation of "capability" adjectives by the suffix *-able*.

(2.11) a. *un(lockable)* 'not able to be locked'
      b. *(unlock)able* 'able to be unlocked'

As in (2.10c), the brackets in (2.11) indicate the **scope** of the operations – that is to say, which parts of the representation *un-* and *-able* operate on. In (2.11a), *un-* operates on *lockable*, but *-able* operates only on *lock*. In (2.11b), *un-* operates only on *lock* and *-able* operates on *unlock*. The differences in meaning that arise as a result of these differences in scope do not just result in *unlockable* being ambiguous: the same bracketing will yield corresponding pairs of meanings for *unbendable, undoable, unfoldable, unstickable* and a number of others.

In syntax too there can be differences in meaning depending on the order in which operations apply. (2.12) is ambiguous for essentially the same reason as *unlockable*: we can think of it as admitting two possible "bracketings", one in which it means that the speaker went two days without sleeping, and another in which it means that the speaker did not sleep continuously for two days.

(2.12) I didn't sleep for two days.

Syntactically, the difference between these two readings is that *for two days* can be treated either as an adjunct or as a complement to *sleep*. In the former case, the meaning that arises is the same as that for the sentence *For two days, I didn't sleep*; in the latter case, the meaning is *It is not the case that I slept for two days*.

Once again, the fact that an ambiguity arises in the interpretation of this sentence is not a one-off fact about (2.12). Corresponding pairs of meanings arise for other sentences that involve a prepositional phrase that could be either an adjunct or a complement. (2.13) presents additional examples.

(2.13) a. I won't be in town until 4 o'clock.
      b. I refuse to see him twice a day.
      c. I agreed to contact her during the committee meeting.

Idioms are exceptions. An expression is an **idiom** if its meaning is not compositional: that is to say, if it cannot be worked out by considering the meanings of its parts and how those parts are put together. Classic examples in English are expressions such as *browned off*, *see eye to eye* or *kick the bucket*. These simply have to be learned as wholes (see Grant and Bauer 2004 for more discussion). In a sense, individual words can also be thought of as idioms: the best we can do with a typical one-morpheme word is to pair it with its meaning. That is also true of words like *greenhouse* or *greengrocer* – although these are clearly composed from two separate parts that have independent existences as words, the meaning of the whole is not predictable from the meaning of the parts.

2.3 Synonymy

Synonymy is equivalence of sense. The nouns *mother, mom* and *mum* are synonyms of each other. When a single word in a sentence is replaced by a **synonym** – a word equivalent in sense – then the literal meaning of the sentence is not changed: *My mother's/mum's/mom's family name was Christie.* Sociolinguistic differences (such as the fact that *mum* and *mom* are informal, and used respectively in British English and North American English) are irrelevant here because they do not affect the propositional content of the sentence.

Sentences with the same meaning are called **paraphrases**. (2.14a) and (2.14b) are paraphrases, differing only by substitution of the synonyms *impudent* and *cheeky*.

(2.14) a. Andy is impudent.
        b. Andy is cheeky.
        c. Andy is impudent $\Rightarrow$ Andy is cheeky
        d. Andy is cheeky $\Rightarrow$ Andy is impudent
        e. *Andy is impudent but he isn't cheeky.
        f. *Andy is cheeky but he isn't impudent.

(2.14a) entails (2.14b), assuming that we are talking about the same Andy at the same point in time: when (2.14a) is true, (2.14b) is also true. However, to establish that a relation of paraphrase holds, we need the entailment to go both ways: (2.14b) must also entail (2.14a). That is the case here, as shown by the entailment relations in (2.14c) and (2.14d), and by the fact that both (2.14e) and (2.14f) are contradictions.

If you are attempting to produce a semantic description of English and you are able to find paraphrases such as (2.14a) and (2.14b), which contain a different adjective but are otherwise identical, then you have evidence that these two adjectives are synonyms of one another. Alternatively, if someone else's description of the semantics of English lists *impudent* and *cheeky* as synonyms, that would tell you that they predict that sentences such as (2.14a) and (2.14b) are paraphrases of one another, and that the corresponding sentences of the form (2.14e) and (2.14f) will be contradictions. Indeed, if two sentences of the form (2.14e) and (2.14f) are both contradictions, that also constitutes evidence that the adjectives in question are synonymous.

The notion of paraphrase depends upon entailment, as it is defined as a two-way entailment between the sentences. Entailments indicate sense relations between words, and sense relations indicate the entailment potentials of words.

How can we find paraphrases? Well, we must observe language in use, and potentially invent test sentences to try to show whether or not particular entailments are present. The examples in (2.15) show how the conjunction *so* can be used in test sentences for entailment.

(2.15)   a.   You said Andy is cheeky, so that means he is impudent.
         b.   You said Andy is impudent, so that means he is cheeky.

So generally signals that an inference is being made. When we are dealing with sentences out of context, as in cases where it does not matter who "Andy" is, then the inferences are entailments rather than guesses based on our knowledge of the situation or of the character of a particular Andy.

People who accept (2.15a) as a reasonable argument are accepting, tacitly at least, that *Andy is cheeky* entails that 'Andy is impudent'. Similarly, people who accept (2.15b) as reasonable are accepting that *Andy is impudent* entails that 'Andy is cheeky'. If both of the arguments are accepted as reasonable, then we have the required two-way entailment and we can conclude that the adjectives are synonymous. (That said, it is possible that people will reject one or other of these arguments for reasons that are unrelated to the entailments of the sentence, for instance because there is a difference in register between *cheeky* and *impudent* and it might seem odd to interchange these freely in actual utterances.)

Other pairs of synonymous adjectives include *silent* and *noiseless*, *brave* and *courageous*, and *polite* and *courteous*. It is important to stress that the two-way entailment pattern discussed above is required for synonymy. *Enormous* and *big* are not synonyms: although *The building is enormous* entails that *The building is big*, the reverse is not true, in that the building could be big without being enormous. Hence the relation of synonymy does not hold.

Synonymy is also present in other word classes, as illustrated in (2.15). And, as shown in the *mother* example, it is not restricted to pairs of words: the triplet *sofa*, *settee* and *couch* are all synonymous. The critical evidence for this would be that any two members of that triplet enter into the kind of two-way entailment relation that is characteristic of pairs of synonyms. In fact, because of the way entailment works, synonymy is a **transitive relation**: that is to say, if *a* is a synonym of *b* and *b* is a synonym of *c*, then *a* must also be a synonym of *c*.[2]

(2.15)   truck   lorry   (nouns)
         depart   leave   (verbs)

quickly   fast   (adverbs)
outside   without   (prepositions)

2.4 Complementarity, antonymy, converseness and incompatibility

Certain pairs of adjectives, such as *moving* and *stationary*, not only apply to a broad class of objects but also divide that class, without remainder, into two non-overlapping sets. Everything that is capable of moving or being stationary – presumably any physical objects – is, at a given point in time, either moving or stationary. Some other adjectives that divide their relevant domains in this way are listed in (2.16).

(2.16)   same   different
         right   wrong
         true   false
         intact   damaged
         connected   disconnected

These are pairs of **complementary** terms – so called because the complement of things that are not described by one term are described by the other. That is to say, they give rise to a pattern of entailments illustrated in (2.17).

(2.17)   a.   Maude's is the same as yours.
         b.   Maude's is different from yours.
         c.   (2.17a) ⟹ (not-2.17b), (not-2.17a) ⟹ (2.17b), (2.17b) ⟹ (not-2.17a), (not-2.17b) ⟹ (2.17a)

Assuming that all the people and possessions in (2.17a) are the same as those in (2.17b), all the entailments listed in (2.17c) follow. When (2.17a) is true, (2.17b) must be false, and vice versa, simply because if two things are the same they are not different, and if they are different they are not the same.

Similarly to the case of synonymy, we can take (2.17a) and (2.17b) as evidence for two paraphrase pairs – that is to say, pairs of sentences that express the same proposition. (2.17a) is a paraphrase of the negation of (2.17b) ("Maude's is not different from yours") and (2.17b) is a paraphrase of the negation of (2.17a). Thus, complementaries can be viewed as negative synonyms. There is a slight difference with the synonymy case discussed in Section 2.3, in that the sentence frame has had to change between (2.17a) and (2.17b) – we've replaced *the same as* with *different from* – so we could think of these two phrases as being complementaries, rather than just *same* and *different*, but this doesn't have any particular semantic significance.

Another relevant sense relation, weaker than complementarity, is that of **antonymy**. Although this term is sometimes employed to mean any kind of "oppositeness", here we follow the practice of most semanticists by applying it to one particular sort of opposition, exemplified by the adjectives *noisy* and *silent*, as in (2.18).

(2.18)   a.   The street was noisy.
        b.   The street was silent.
        c.   (2.18a) $\Rightarrow$ (not-2.18b), (2.18b) $\Rightarrow$ (not-2.18a)
        d.   ~~(not-2.18a) $\Rightarrow$ (2.18b), (not-2.18b) $\Rightarrow$ (2.18a)~~

Antonymy is defined by the pattern of entailments shown in (2.18c): if we know that (2.18a) is true then we know that (2.18b) is false (assuming that we're referring to the same street at the same point in time), and if we know that (2.18b) is true then we know that (2.18a) is false. Both of these entailments go from a positive sentence to a negative one: *noisy* entails *not silent*, and *silent* entails *not noisy*. However, for antonymy, we do not get the entailments in (2.18d), which is why these have been scored out. This is because, unlike the case of complementaries, there is middle ground between what *noisy* denotes and what *silent* denotes: to say that something is "not noisy" is not to say that it is silent, and to say that it is "not silent" is not to say that it is noisy.

There are many pairs of antonyms: *happy* and *sad*, *full* and *empty*, *early* and *late*, and so on. It is not a coincidence that it is easier to find pairs of antonyms than it is to find synonyms or complementaries. Synonyms can be thought of as something of a luxury: given that two synonyms (such as *courteous* and *polite*) give rise to the same entailments, we could really do without one of them, at least as far as the transmission of information is concerned. They are perhaps tolerated because they enable us to communicate more expressively and in a stylistically and sociolinguistically richer fashion. For similar reasons, it is something of a luxury to have both members of a complementary pair provided in our language: we could get away with just having one and using negation to convey the other (instead of *false* we could simply say *not true* or *untrue*, and so on). However, this will not work with antonyms: to say that something is *full* is more than just saying that it is *not empty*.

A general feature of the adjectives that form antonym pairs is that there is also a sense relation between their comparative forms. Comparatives are formed by the suffix *-er* for some adjectives (*thicker*, *poorer*, *humbler*) or more generally by the construction "*more* + adjective" (*more patient*, *more obstinate*). The comparative forms of an antonym pair of adjectives exhibit a sense relation called **converseness**, illustrated in (2.19).

(2.19) a. Large US states are richer than many countries.
        b. Many countries are poorer than large US states.
        c. (2.19a ⇒ 2.19b), (2.19b ⇒ 2.19a)

The entailment pattern in (2.19c) defines converseness: starting with (2.19a), if we replace one comparative with the other and "turn the expression round" syntactically, by exchanging the position of the noun phrases, we obtain a paraphrase, (2.19b). We can thus think of converses as something like a version of synonyms that also require the reordering of noun phrases.

Converseness is also present in other word classes, including nouns (such as *parent (of)* and *child (of)*), verbs (such as *precede* and *follow*) and prepositions (such as *above* and *below*). In each of these cases, if we have two entities X and Y, and X stands in one of these relations to Y, it must be the case that Y stands in the converse relationship to X (for example, if X is *above* Y, then Y is *below* X, and vice versa).

Just as synonymy is not restricted to pairs of items, neither is antonymy. We can often identify sets of terms for which any two members are antonyms: we can say that these sets exhibit **incompatibility**. For instance, we can consider a set of colour adjectives such as {*black, blue, green, yellow, red, white, grey*} to be incompatible, in that if we say something is "blue" it follows automatically that it is not black, green, yellow, etc. – assuming that we are dealing with objects with a single predominant colour. Similarly, a set of nouns denoting shapes, such as {*triangle, circle, square*}, might also exhibit incompatibility: if something is "a triangle" it is not a circle or a square, and so on. A set has incompatibility if every member of the set exhibits antonymy with every other member of the set, so the diagnostics for incompatibility will be essentially the same as for antonymy.

2.5 Hyponymy

The relation of **hyponymy** is concerned with the labelling of subcategories of a word's denotation: what kind of Xs are there, and what different kinds of entities count as Ys? For instance, a *house* is one kind of *building*, and a *factory* and a *church* are other kinds of *building*. A *building* is in turn one kind of *structure*; a *dam* is another kind of structure.

The pattern of entailment that defines hyponymy is illustrated in (2.20).

(2.20) a. There's a house next to the gate.
        b. There's a building next to the gate.
        c. (2.20a) ⇒ (2.20b), (2.20b) ⇒ (2.20a)

If it is true that there is a house next to the gate, then (with respect to the same gate at the same moment in time) it must also be true that there is a building next to the gate; it cannot be otherwise. The reverse entailment does not hold: if it is true that there is a building next to the gate, it need not be the case that there is a house there (the building could be a factory or a church or any other kind of building). This is indicated by the scored-out part of (2.20c).

Terminologically, we can say that *building* is a **superordinate** of *house*, and of other nouns that label specific kinds of building. *House* is a **hyponym** of *building*. (Superordinates are sometimes called "hypernyms" or "hyperonyms", but we will stick with the less easily confusable term here.)

We can generalise the pattern shown in (2.20): a sentence containing a hyponym of a given superordinate entails the corresponding sentence in which the hyponym has been replaced by the superordinate. The reverse is not true. However, this generalisation is not entirely watertight: for instance, it breaks down if the sentence is negative. (2.21) shows corresponding negative sentences for the examples in (2.20), and as we can see, the direction of entailment is reversed here.

(2.21)   a.   There isn't a house next to the gate.
          b.   There isn't a building next to the gate.
          c.   ~~(2.21a) ⇒ (2.21b)~~, (2.21b) ⇒ (2.21a)

Incidentally, this highlights the fact that there being a building by the gate is a necessary condition for there to be a house by the gate: if there is no building there, there cannot be a house there. Intuitively it is reasonable to say that 'building' is a component of the meaning of *house*: a *house* is a 'building for living in'.

2.5.1 Hierarchies of hyponyms

House is a hyponym of the superordinate *building*, but *building* is in turn a hyponym of *structure*, and in its turn *structure* is a hyponym of *thing*. A superordinate at a given level can itself be a hyponym of a superordinate at a higher level, as shown in Figure 2.1.

The hyponymy relation passes through intermediate levels in the hierarchy, which means that *house* is not only a hyponym of *building* but also of *structure* and *thing*. Similarly, *thing* is also a superordinate of all the words on lines that can be traced down from it in the hierarchy, as shown in Figure 2.2. (This means, incidentally, that we don't have to worry about whether there are intermediate levels between *structure* and *thing*, such as perhaps *artefact*: the hyponymy relations that we've stated will still hold.)

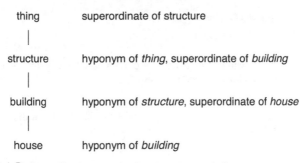

Figure 2.1 Superordinates can be hyponyms and vice versa

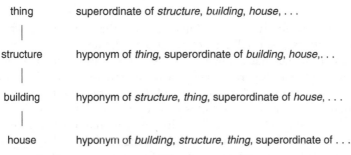

Figure 2.2 Hyponymy passes through intermediate levels

As a result, a hierarchy of this kind guarantees numerous inferences. If someone who is speaking the truth tells us about a house, we know, with certainty and without having to ask, that the entity in question is also a building and a structure and a thing (and everything that is said about that house could also be said of a building and of a structure and of a thing).

The ellipses (...) in Figure 2.2 are used because the diagram shows only a fragment of the hierarchy. There are other kinds of things besides structures; there are other kinds of structures besides buildings; there are other kinds of buildings besides houses. And there are also words that are hyponyms of *house* (for example, *cottage* and *bungalow*).

High up the hierarchy, the senses of words are rather general and lacking in detail, which has the consequence that these words denote many different kinds of entity. At successively lower levels, the meanings are more detailed and therefore the words denote narrower ranges of things, as illustrated in Figure 2.3.

Notice that the meaning of a hyponym is given in Figure 2.3 as the meaning of its immediate superordinate elaborated by a modifier

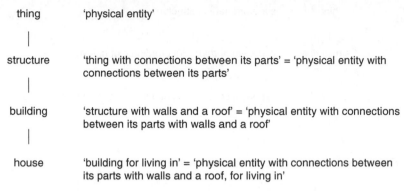

Figure 2.3 Hyponym senses get successively more detailed

(for example, 'for living in'). This captures the essential insight that a hyponym is a special case of its superordinate: it's an instance of its superordinate that happens to have certain properties that not all instances of that superordinate share. In practice, not all hyponym definitions of this kind are at all useful, because we often encounter circularity. For instance, a dog is a type of animal, but it's difficult to describe what type of animal it is without using the word 'dog' or some related word such as 'canine' – it is, in effect, an 'animal that is a dog'.

Hyponym hierarchies exist not only for nouns but also for other parts of speech such as verbs and adjectives. *Amble* is a hyponym of *walk* which in turn is a hyponym of *move*; *(made of) oak* is a hyponym of *wooden*, and so on. Hierarchies of this kind are potentially vast. Miller and Fellbaum (1991) report on the development of WordNet, a systematic database of English word meanings, which by 1991 contained entries for more than 54,000 different words, and at the time of writing (2016) contains more than 155,000. In creating the database, they found that a hyponym hierarchy with twenty-six high-level superordinates (*time, plant, animal*, and so on) 'provides a place for every English noun' (1991: 204). Figure 2.4 represents a tiny fraction of the WordNet noun hierarchy, featuring just seven of their twenty-six superordinates (and omitting the vast majority of their hyponyms). Note that some entities appear twice in this hierarchy: we distinguish two senses of *person* (corresponding roughly to 'human' and 'psychological individual') and two senses of *animal* (corresponding roughly to 'living thing that is not a plant' and 'living thing that is not a plant or a human').

Other sense relations can occur within a hyponym hierarchy. We might expect the hyponyms of a given superordinate to be linked by a relation of incompatibility – although this is not guaranteed, and

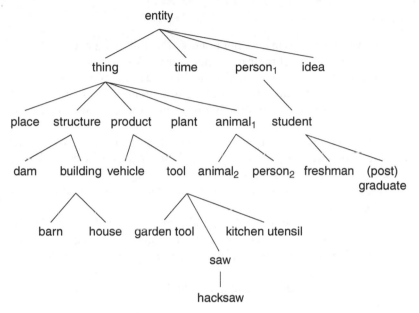

Figure 2.4 Part of the hyponym hierarchy of English nouns

depends on how we set up the hierarchy. In principle we might assume that *house* and *factory* are different hyponyms of *building*, and therefore something that is a *house* is not a *factory*, but this does not follow automatically from the definition of hyponymy that we have been working with here. For instance, if *house* and *dwelling* are synonyms, then both are hyponyms of *building*, but they are clearly not incompatible.

Summary

In this chapter, we discussed the notion of entailment and its relevance to semantics. Based on this, we were able to define various distinct sense relations that can obtain between expressions in a language: synonymy, antonymy, complementarity, converseness, incompatibility and hyponymy. In the process of giving the semantic description of a language, entailments between sentences are the evidence for sense relations between words. Going the other way, the sense relations in a semantic description indicate the entailment potentials of words. The resulting entailments are crucial not only for the effectiveness of communication within a language, but also for our ability to learn the semantics of a language through the use of language itself.

Exercises

1. The word *dishonest* means 'not honest'. The following five words also have 'not' as part of their meaning: *distrust, disregard, disprove, dislike, dissuade.* Write a two-word gloss for the meaning of each, similar to the one given for *dishonest.* Thinking of sentences for the words will probably help. Use the term "scope" (introduced in Section 2.2) to describe the difference.

2. Here is an unsatisfactory attempt to explain the meaning of *not good enough: not good* means 'bad or average'; *enough* means 'sufficiently'; so *not good enough* means 'sufficiently bad or average'.
   With the aid of brackets, explain why the phrase actually means 'inadequate'.

3. Someone once said to me "You and I are well suited. We don't like the same things." The context indicated (and I checked by asking) that the speaker meant to convey that we are well suited because the things we don't like are the same: but the sentence is in principle ambiguous. Explain the ambiguity, and comment on unambiguous alternatives.

4. Which of the following sentences entail which?

   (a)   The students liked the course.
   (b)   The students loved the course
   (c)   The rain stopped.
   (d)   The rain ceased.

5. Provide example sentences and write out a pattern of entailments (comparable to (2.14a–d)) that establishes *soundless, silent* and *noiseless* as synonymous.

6. Are *awake* and *asleep* complementaries? Give reasons for your answer. Whether you have answered yes or no, how would you include *half-awake, half-asleep* and *dozy* in an account of the meanings of *awake* and *asleep?*

7. The hyponyms of *footwear* include *shoes, sneakers, trainers, sandals, slippers, boots* and *galoshes.* Draw up a hyponym hierarchy for these words. Is *footwear* the superordinate that you use for all of the hyponyms, or are there other alternatives?

Recommendations for reading

Cruse (2011) provides a thorough discussion of oppositeness in meaning, as well as hyponymy. Lappin (2001) provides a good article-length introduction to formal semantics, and Saeed (2015) complements this by dealing in greater detail with some relevant topics. Quite a lot can be learnt about sense relations as applied to particular word classes by looking through the relevant sections of major grammars of English, such as Quirk et al. (1985) and Huddleston and Pullum (2002).

Notes

1. The entailment relation can be written in various other ways: the symbol ⊢ is sometimes used for the purpose. "p ⊢ q" also symbolises that p entails q.
2. Among the other sense relations discussed in this chapter, hyponymy is also transitive: if *a* is a hyponym of *b* and *b* is a hyponym of *c*, then *a* is a hyponym of *c*. Antonymy, complementarity, converseness and incompatibility are not transitive. For instance, if *a* is an antonym of *b*, then *b* is an antonym of *a*, but *a* is not an antonym of itself.

3 Nouns

Overview

Nouns form a majority of words in the vocabulary of English, and typically denote entities with rich and complex sets of properties. In addition to the properties acquired by nouns' entry into hyponymy relations (as discussed in Section 2.5), nouns also exhibit a sense relation which we can call the *has*-relation: the "things" denoted by some nouns have parts, which may figure in the nouns' meaning. For example, a *square* has four sides of equal length and four 90° angles, and in saying what a *square* is, one cannot avoid talking about its four sides and right angles. The chapter ends with a discussion of meaning differences between count and mass nouns: that is, between those nouns that are treated in English as though they have distinguishable parts and those which are treated as though they do not.

3.1 The *has*-relation

The everyday words *square*, *circle* and *triangle* are also technical terms in geometry, where they have tight definitions. For example, a closed, straight-sided figure is a triangle if and only if it has exactly three sides. This underpins entailments such as *that figure is a triangle* ⟹ *that figure has three sides*. For many words, however, we can only be sure that all the parts are there if we think in terms of prototypes. **Prototypes** are clear, central members of the denotation of a word.

Think of what you might advise a child drawing a face to put in: probably eyes, a nose and a mouth. How about a child drawing a house? Perhaps a roof, a door (or doors) and windows. Among the things denoted by the English word *face*, the prototypical ones have eyes, a nose and a mouth. The face of a Cyclops, with a single central eye, is a *face*, but not a prototypical one. Similarly, the Blackhouse of Arnol on the Isle of Lewis is a house but has no windows, and in that respect is non-prototypical as a *house* as far as contemporary English usage is concerned. The information that needs to be built into meaning postulates (see Section 2.1.1) to reflect these particular semantic facts is listed in (3.1).

(3.1) A prototypical face has two eyes, a nose and a mouth.
       A prototypical house has a roof, a door and windows.

Prototypical faces and houses may have other features besides these, of course. Importantly, there are also numerous features that many real faces and houses have that are not likely to be present in prototypical faces and houses (say a goatee, or a carport, respectively).

The *has*-**relation** makes certain entailments available from statements about nouns. Some examples are given in (3.2).

(3.2) a. *That figure is a triangle* ⇒ 'That figure has three sides'
       b. *The building on the corner is a house* ⇒ 'If it is prototypical, then the building on the corner has windows'
       c. *The child drew a face* ⇒ 'If the face was prototypical, then the child drew a mouth'

In Section 2.1, entailments were introduced as guarantees; for example (3.2a) that is still appropriate, but for the other examples in (3.2) we've weakened the entailments by making them conditional on prototypicality. This is necessary because average English words are not as tightly defined as technical words like *triangle*. But it is also useful, because for many nouns there are very few essential properties, but plenty of prototypical ones.

This point has been argued by a number of influential thinkers about language, so I want to dwell on it for a moment. We can legitimately say that a geometrical figure must have exactly three sides in order to be called a *triangle*, and this entails that anything (correctly) called a *triangle* has exactly three sides. However, for lots of words, it is very difficult to identify any obligatory properties. Wittgenstein (1953) famously discussed the meaning of *game*, and argued that there were no features that characterised everything that could be called a *game*: not all games involve competition, or skill, or physical ability; not all games have rules; not all games have playing pieces or a scoring system. So by this token, knowing that something "is a game" doesn't tell you anything about the *has*-relations that it possesses. This approach has motivated the idea that word meanings are organised (at least in part) around prototypes rather than obligatory properties – an idea called "prototype theory" and particularly associated with Eleanor Rosch and colleagues.

Similarly, although a prototypical *house* has *windows, doors* and a *roof*, a house which has no windows, or no doors, or which loses its roof, doesn't definitively cease to be a house. Hence, to call something a *house* is not to guarantee that it has these features. It follows that the statement in (3.2b) doesn't tell us very much with absolute certainty about the building on the corner: it doesn't tell us that it must have windows, or that it must have doors, or that it must have a roof. However, it does rather strongly suggest (in the absence of indications to the contrary) that the building in question has windows, doors and a roof. We would like our semantics to reflect that, and for that reason we're going to have to make some assumptions about prototypicality. (Later, in the discussion of the *has*-relation and hyponymy, we'll see one of the limitations of this approach.)

3.1.1 Pragmatic inferences from the has-relation

The *has*-relation, as applied to prototypes, is the basis for some of our pragmatic expectations in language use. This can be seen in the switch from indefinite to definite articles. A noun phrase that first introduces its referent into a conversation is usually indefinite (for instance, in English, marked by the use of an indefinite article, *a* or *an*). However, subsequent mentions of the same referent will usually involve a definite noun phrase (for instance, marked by the definite article *the*), as in (3.3).

(3.3) a. A: "I've bought a house."
           B: "Where's the house?" / * "Where's a house?"
       b. C: "I drew a face."
           D: "I like the face you drew." / ?"I like a face you drew."

However, if the thing that has been introduced prototypically has a part, then that part can be referred to on first mention by means of a definite noun phrase, as seen in (3.4).

(3.4) a. A: "I've bought a house."
           B: "Did you have the roof surveyed?" / *"Did you have a roof surveyed?"
       b. C: "I drew a face."
           D: "Where's the nose?" / *"Where's a nose?"

There will be more on the use of definite and indefinite articles in Chapter 10.

3.1.2 Hyponymy and the has-relation

These two semantic relations should not be confused: hyponymy is about categories being grouped under superordinate terms (for example, *tandems, ATBs, tourers* and *racers* are kinds of *bicycle*, and *bicycles, unicycles* and *tricycles* are kinds of *cycle*), whereas the *has*-relation concerns parts that members of categories have (for instance, a prototypical *cycle* has *wheels*, a *frame, handlebars, pedals*, and so on). It would obviously be false to say that "a cycle has tandems" or "handlebars are a type of cycle", so it's clear that hyponymy and the *has*-relation are not the same thing.

Nevertheless, these two relations are linked, in that hyponyms "inherit" the parts that their superordinates have (Miller and Fellbaum 1991: 206). A convenient example from geometry would be that *square, rectangle, kite, parallelogram, rhombus* and *trapezium* are all hyponyms of *quadrilateral*. By definition, a *quadrilateral* has exactly four sides. This relationship is inherited by all the hyponyms of *quadrilateral*. If those hyponyms were themselves superordinates to other hyponyms, those hyponyms would also inherit the property of "having exactly four sides". For instance, *trapezium* is ambiguous between two meanings: a shape with one pair of parallel sides (known in North America as a *trapezoid*) and a shape with no parallel sides (known outside North America as a *general irregular quadrilateral*). If we take both these terms to be hyponyms of a vaguely defined notion of *trapezium*, then both will inherit any *has*-relations that apply to a *trapezium*, as well as any *has*-relations that apply to its superordinate *quadrilateral* (and any *has*-relations that apply to its superordinate, perhaps *polygon*, and so on).

This inheritance works well for terms with clear definitions, such as mathematical shapes, but it becomes a bit tricky when we are dealing with prototypes. It is not generally true that the prototype for a hyponym has all the features that the prototype of its superordinate has. If we take the *cycle* example, it's true that the prototype *bicycle* also has the features of the prototype *cycle*, namely *wheels*, a *frame, handlebars, pedals*. However, the prototype *unicycle* does not have *handlebars* (and it would be odd to say that it has *wheels*).

As a general observation, this will apply not only to the *has*-relation but also to other properties. A classic example is that a property of a prototypical *bird* is that it "can fly". This property is inherited by most of the hyponyms of *bird*, but of course not all: *penguin* is a hyponym of *bird* and the prototypical *penguin* cannot fly. In fact, there's no reason to suppose that a given property of a prototypical superordinate will be inherited by most of its hyponyms: that's really an accidental fact about language. If we had 10,000 words for different kinds of penguin, they would all be hyponyms of *bird*, but it wouldn't alter the fact that a prototypical *bird* can fly and a *penguin* cannot.

In short, then, we can think of hyponyms inheriting obligatory properties, including *has*-relations, from their superordinates. As far as prototypical properties are concerned, this is not guaranteed. Nevertheless, it might be reasonable to think that prototypical properties of superordinates are somewhat likely to be inherited by at least some of (the prototypical instances of) the corresponding hyponyms.

3.1.3 Parts can have parts

Just as hyponyms can themselves have hyponyms, so the parts of an object – the things that that object *has* – can themselves have parts. We could say, for instance, that *a suburb has houses, a house has windows, a window has panes*, and so on.

As far as the properties of these parts are concerned, remember that again we're dealing with the *has*-relation rather than hyponymy. Even if properties are obligatory for a whole, they need not be obligatory of its parts. A *square* obligatorily has four sides and four corners, but it is not true that "each side has four corners" or "each corner has four sides".

3.1.4 Spatial parts

A prototypical *thing*, such as a rock, can be said to have a *top*, a *bottom* (or *base*), *sides*, and a *front* and *back*. Although not all things prototypically have all these spatial parts (for reasons discussed in Section 3.1.2), very many different kinds of thing do – *windows, heads, feet, buses* and *trees* to name but a few.

Spatial part words are often deictic: that is to say, their meaning is tied to the context of utterance. For that reason, pragmatics enters into the interpretation of such words. What counts as the *front* of a rock is usually the part facing the speaker, while the *back* of a rock faces away from the speaker. What counts as the *bottom* and *top* of the rock depends upon which way up the rock happens to be lying at the time of utterance. However, a lot of things have a particular orientation: a *bus*, for instance, has a *front* and a *back* that are intrinsic to its structure irrespective of where the speaker is standing, and a *top* (its roof) and a *bottom* (and *sides*), terms which still correspond to the same parts of the bus whether it is on its wheels or on its side. The list in Table 3.1 gives further examples of this kind.

In practice, the situation is even more complicated than this. Firstly, although the speaker normally behaves as the deictic centre ("I call this part of the rock *the front* because it is the nearest part to me"), it's possible to behave as though the hearer is the deictic centre, and talk about parts of an object in terms of proximity to them ("I call this part of the rock *the front* because it is the nearest part to you"). Secondly, for many objects with an intrinsic orientation, it's still possible to be

Table 3.1 Examples of two kinds of spatial parts

Having inherent spatial parts	*Having spatial parts only deictically*
people	balls
houses	planets (in the talk of amateurs looking through a telescope)
trees (top, base, sides)	trees (front, back)
hills (top, base, sides)	hills (front, back)
animals	
pianos	

speaker-centric – or indeed hearer-centric. Suppose that there is a chair in the middle of the room and you are standing two metres behind it (according to its intrinsic orientation) and facing towards it, while I'm standing two metres to the left of it (from your point of view) and also facing towards it. I now say "Please place a coin in front of the chair". (This is admittedly a very odd request, so you might surmise that I'm doing a psycholinguistic experiment.) There are three separate ways in which you could interpret that instruction, depending on whether you interpret *in front of* to mean "in the region adjacent to the front of the chair, according to its intrinsic structure", "in the region adjacent to the front of the chair, from the speaker's point of view" or "in the region adjacent to the front of the chair, from the hearer's point of view". How we resolve this kind of ambiguity in practice is still an open research question (see Johannsen and De Ruiter 2013 for discussion).

3.1.5 Ends and beginnings

Long thin things have *ends*, and sometimes two different kinds of *end* are distinguished, *beginnings* and *ends*. A list of some of the things that prototypically have *ends* is given in (3.5).

(3.5)   ropes
        (pieces of) string
        ships (though mariners have special words for them, *stern* and *bow*)
        roads
        trains
        planks

Nouns denoting periods of time have *beginnings* and *ends*. They also have *middles*. Some examples are listed in (3.6a). Similarly, while the words in (3.6b) do not denote concrete entities, they nevertheless refer to events and processes that are located in time and space: it would be reasonable to wonder when and where these things took place. They can also have *beginnings*, *middles* and *ends*. Later we will see how this relates to verb meanings.

(3.6)   a.   *day, week, month, era, term, semester, century*
        b.   *conversation, demonstration, ceremony, meal, reception, process*

3.1.6 Body parts

The body is a particularly rich source of metaphors (see Chapter 9), and for that reason, words for body parts are common in English (and many other languages) to describe many different kinds of object. If you are told that the mountain at Machu Picchu looks like a face, you might reasonably expect it to have parts corresponding to a mouth, nose, chin, eyes and cheeks, without invoking any specialised knowledge of anatomy. The body part labels *head, neck, foot* and *mouth* are used to label parts of a wide range of things: for example, a *mountain* has a *head* and a *foot, bottles* have *necks, caves* and *rivers* have *mouths.* Presumably this indicates a human tendency to interpret and label the world by analogy with what we understand most intimately, our own bodies. However, of course, the kinds of *has*-relations that are exhibited by these terms in the context of a body do not reliably carry over to these metaphorical cases: while *mouths* have *lips, rivers* and *caves* do not.

3.2 Count nouns and mass nouns

In the grammar of English, there is a clear distinction between **count nouns**, exemplified by *loaf* and *coin*, and **mass nouns**, exemplified by *bread* and *money.* Mass nouns are those that resist being quantified with numbers and plural suffixes, or the word *many*, or the singular indefinite article *a*, while count nouns are those that can be quantified in this way. The whole noun vocabulary divides into words that are almost always count nouns (such as *garment*), those that are almost always mass nouns (such as *clothing*), and those which can be used as either (such as *cake*). Table 3.2 gives some examples of acceptable and unacceptable usages. (There are also some marginal cases here in which mass nouns can be coerced into a countable use, as for instance when *bread* is taken to denote 'distinct variety of bread'.)

Count nouns denote distinguishable whole entities, like beans or people or shirts. They can be counted. Mass nouns are quantified by the word *much.* They denote undifferentiated substance, such as dough or water or lava.

Table 3.2 Distinguishing between count and mass nouns

Count nouns	Mass nouns
This is a loaf.	?This is a bread.
This is a coin.	*This is a money.
How many loaves are there?	?How many breads are there?
How many coins are there?	*How many monies are there?
a large number of loaves	?a large number of breads
a large number of coins	*a large number of monies
six loaves	?six breads
six coins	*six monies
?some loaf	some bread
*some coin	some money
some loaves	?some breads
some coins	?some monies
*How much loaves are there?	How much bread is there?
*How much coins are there?	How much money is there?

Table 3.2 shows that the difference between count nouns and mass nouns is partly a matter of how the speaker chooses to portray reality. What is out there in the world is pretty much the same regardless of whether you are referring to a *loaf* or to *bread*; likewise, the denotation of the word *coins* (and *banknotes* or *bills*) is pretty much the same as that of the word *money*. However, count nouns portray what we are talking about as consisting of individually distinct wholes, while talking about the same thing with mass nouns represents it as homogeneous, undifferentiated "stuff".

It is certainly not the case that when people use mass nouns to talk about *clothing* or *scenery* that they become incapable of distinguishing shirts from socks, or incapable of seeing boundaries between lakes and mountains. They are merely treating the whole as though it were not quantifiable by counting its constituent parts.

Hyponymy (and incompatibility) exists among mass nouns just as among count nouns: *velvet, corduroy, denim* and so on are incompatible hyponyms of the mass noun *cloth*, and are themselves mass nouns. In principle, we might expect mass nouns not to enter into *has*-relations, because homogeneous substance is not separable into distinct parts: but this is perhaps not a clear-cut issue, simply because (as remarked above) whether we treat something as mass or count doesn't necessarily say a great deal about its physical reality. If we agree that *cloth has threads*, then this is a *has*-relation involving a mass noun, and it is inherited by the hyponyms of *cloth* in the usual fashion.

Summary

In this chapter we have considered some of the characteristic properties of nouns, with particular emphasis on the *has*-relation and the interplay between this and other sense relations. We have seen that the *has*-relation is a potentially powerful tool for learning about the entailments of hyponyms of nouns, but that this only holds reliably when we are dealing with obligatory properties, and is only a (perhaps helpful) indication when we are dealing with prototypical properties. We also considered the distinction between count nouns and mass nouns as a way of portraying the world: labelling with a mass noun treats what is referred to as a homogeneous substance without distinct parts, and this has consequences for how we can talk about this referent. However, the distinction between mass nouns and count nouns does not correspond to a crisp distinction between two kinds of thing that exist in the world, but rather between two distinct ways in which we can relate to those things through language. In Chapter 5 we will see that similar distinctions can be made in the case of verbs.

Exercises

1. What parts does a prototype *shoe* have? Do those parts have parts?
2. If we wanted to describe the meanings of some spatial part words, we might say something like this:

   "The *top* of a thing is one of its *sides*, the side that is uppermost. The *bottom* of a thing is one of its *sides*, the side that is down. The *front* is one of the *sides*, the side that faces forwards. The *back* is one of its *sides*, the side that faces away from the front."

   If this description is correct, what sense relations hold between the words *side, top, bottom, front* and *back*? Give reasons to support your answer.
3. *Paper, glass* and *cheese* are ambiguous between a count sense and a mass sense.

   a. Devise a pair of example sentences for each of them that clearly brings out the count–mass difference.
   b. Find some hyponyms for each of the words in each of its senses. Use these to comment on the systematic difference in meaning between the count and mass interpretations of these words.

4. In the question "Have you ever eaten rabbit?", what difference does the lack of an article (*rabbit* instead of *a rabbit*) make to the interpretation of the noun *rabbit*?
5. Why might we interpret *left* differently when we are describing something as being *to the left of the chair* versus *to the left of the stool*?

Recommendations for reading

For prototype theory, Mervis and Rosch (1981) gives a detailed overview of some of the major ideas and their consequences. Johannsen and De Ruiter (2013) report useful work on spatial perspective and frames of reference. Kearns (2011) is an excellent source for more about differences in meaning between mass and count nouns. Imai (2000) reports on an interesting series of experiments on count and mass noun meanings, comparing English- and Japanese-speaking children and adults.

4 Adjectives

Overview

Cruse (2011) notes that adjective meanings are often one-dimensional: think of pairs like *thin–thick*, *fast–slow*, *true–false*, *cool–warm*, *young–old*, and so on. In Chapter 2, we exemplified several important sense relations primarily with respect to adjectives, including synonymy, complementarity, antonymy, incompatibility and converseness, although these relations are applicable to other parts of speech as well. In this chapter we focus on a characteristic of certain adjectives in particular, namely gradability. We also consider how adjective meanings compose with those of the nouns that they modify, and begin to explore how contextual factors bear upon the interpretation of adjectives.

4.1 Gradability

The comparative forms introduced in the discussion of converseness (Section 2.4) exist because of a general property of some adjectives (and adverbs): they are **gradable**. That is to say, the language has ways of expressing different degrees or levels of the qualities that they denote. Some examples of this are given in (4.1), with the relevant indicators of gradability italicised in each case.

(4.1)   Card is thick*er than* paper.
        Showers will be *more* frequent tomorrow.
        He is the rud*est* person I've ever met.
        They are *too* rare to stand any chance of survival.
        Just *how* patient do you have to be?
        The conditions were *very* harsh.

The adjectives in the examples given in (4.1) are all members of antonym pairs. Each denotes a region towards one or the other end of a scale. For instance, there is a scale of thickness, with *thick* denoting values towards one end, *thin* denoting values towards the other end, and a region in between comprising values that are not readily denoted either by *thick* or by *thin*.

Interestingly, such pairs are not entirely symmetrical in how they behave within the language system. For instance, it is often the case that one member of the pair is used to ask neutral questions about values on the scale, while the other member is used to ask questions that signal some particular expectation on the part of the speaker. The classic example is perhaps the pair *young–old*, where *old* is used to ask neutral questions, as in (4.2).

(4.2) a. How old is that footballer?
       b. How young is that footballer?

(4.2b) would be an odd question to ask about a professional football player who appeared to be around thirty years old. It would be acceptable only in contexts in which there was either an expectation that the player in question is young ("That player must be young, but to how extreme an extent is that the case?"), or that that the player should be young ("Is that player really young to the extent reported/required?") By contrast, (4.2a) merely enquires where the footballer is situated on the age scale, and would be coherent whether the player in question was five or fifty years old.

Not all adjectives are gradable: for instance, members of complementary pairs (see Section 2.4) are sometimes resistant to grading. In particular, some of these pairs serve to partition entities into two classes, but do not necessarily distinguish between the entities within those classes as to "how good" they are as exemplars of the adjective. In the case of the pair *connected* and *disconnected*, we could plausibly say that everything that is connected is connected to just the same extent as everything else that is connected; and likewise for the things that are disconnected.

In the case of the pair *same* and *different*, we could make a similar argument: all the things that are *the same as X* are "the same as X" to an equal extent. However, in this case, the argument doesn't apply to the other term, *different*: that might be gradable. It's true to say that neither a lemon nor the Space Shuttle is the same as an orange, but it's also plausible to say that the Space Shuttle is more different from an orange than a lemon is different from an orange. The examples in (4.3) illustrate some adjectives from complementary pairs that seem to demonstrate varying levels of acceptability as gradable adjectives.

(4.3)   a.   *Twins are samer/more same than siblings.
     b.   Dizygotic twins are more different than monozygotic twins.
     b.   *The jury heard evidence that was too false to accept.
     c.   ?That is the rightest answer I have heard today.
     d.   ?How disconnected is this kettle from the power supply?
     e.   ?They left the door very open.

Superlatives, such as *best* and *fastest*, denote extreme ends of scales. This naturally makes them resistant to grading: their position on the scale is not up for negotiation, so attempting to clarify it through modification is unnecessary. Some other adjectives denoting extreme values, such as *freezing*, are similarly resistant to grading, as shown in (4.4) – and when they do appear to be used gradably, it might actually just represent a form of emphasis (as in the case of *very unique*).

(4.4)   a.   *The other team was bester than ours.
     b.   *In the inner city walking is more fastest.
     c.   *The presentation was very excellent.
     d.   ?The weather was too freezing.

Conversely, there are some things that can be done with these extreme adjectives that can't be done with ordinary gradable adjectives. For instance, they can be modified with "maximiser" adverbs such as *absolutely* and *completely*, as shown in (4.5).

(4.5)   a.   *The shrink wrapping was absolutely thin.
     b.   *Her performance was completely good.
     c.   You'll look completely different with your hair restyled.
     d.   What you say is absolutely true.
     e.   Digital sound reproduction is completely impeccable.
     f.   The weather has been absolutely freezing.

4.2 Composing adjectives with nouns

How are noun and adjective meanings put together when an adjective modifies a noun, as in *green bicycles*? In general, this is a deceptively tricky question: here we'll just introduce some of the interesting issues that arise in this area.

Certainly there are many cases in which we can give a fairly simple account of adjective–noun meaning. We could simply say that *green bicycles* denotes all the things that are at once *green* and *bicycles*. This is an idea which we can express in terms of set theory, as sketched in Figure 4.1.

In Figure 4.1, the left-hand oval represents the set of entities denoted

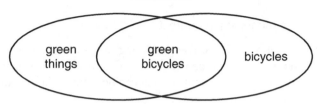

Figure 4.1 Simple cases of an adjective modifying a noun are like the intersection of sets

by *green*, comprising all the green entities that there could be. The right-hand oval represents the set of entities denoted by *bicycle*: that is to say, all bicycles. The intersection of the two ovals encompasses things that are included in both sets: that is, everything that is simultaneously a bicycle and a thing that is green. This seems to correspond satisfactorily with the denotation of the expression *green bicycle*, so this idea of considering the intersection of two sets offers a satisfactory account of how these two meanings are put together. Adjectives that fit this scheme of interpretation are called **intersective** adjectives.

Some adjectives are generally non-intersective: *former* and *future* seem to belong to this category. A *former leader* is not a *leader*, at the time of utterance; a *future star* is not a *star*. In some cases, usages which appear to be non-intersective can be treated as intersective by broadening the denotation of the noun: it seems reasonable to describe *former President* Bill Clinton as *a president of the United States* or *former champion* Lennox Lewis as *a world heavyweight champion*. Adjectives such as *alleged* are non-intersective: an *alleged thief* may or may not be a *thief*.

A more problematic case is *fake*: a *fake Picasso* is, by definition, not a (painting by) Picasso. Adjectives of this kind are sometimes described as "anti-intersective" or "privative": the use of the adjective actually precludes reference to anything falling within the usual denotation of the noun. Yet even to qualify as a *fake Picasso* the painting must have some close resemblance, in some relevant respects, to a *(genuine) Picasso*. If you paint a portrait, even in a Cubist style, it would be odd to describe the result as a *fake Picasso*, unless you make some particular attempt to pass the work off as Picasso's own (such as by writing his name on it). This raises the question of whether we could interpret *Picasso* to denote a larger class of works in some sense "like" the paintings of Picasso, and thus make *fake* intersective too. Lappin (2001) gives a short overview of some proposals in formal semantics for handling non-intersective adjectives of this kind.

4.3 Adjective meanings in context

Further examples of adjectives behaving non-intersectively appear when we take context into consideration. For instance, it is difficult to give a fully intersective account of what can be called relative adjectives (Cruse 2011), such as the examples in (4.6).

(4.6)   a.   Sucrose is a big molecule.
         b.   The swimming pool was the size of a narrow shipping lane.

The problem with offering a fully intersective account of modification with *small*, or *big*, or *wide*, or *narrow*, or any of the many other relative adjectives, is that these adjectives are interpreted relative to the norms of the entities denoted by the noun. It is not the case that *big molecule* denotes the set of things that are molecules and that are "big" among the reference class of things in general. To put it another way, if we define a single absolute threshold for "bigness" in such a way as to make some molecules "big", then everything visible to the naked eye would automatically qualify as "big" too – and this doesn't cohere with how our language is used.

It follows that the same thing could be *big* according to one criterion and *small* according to another. (4.6b) attempts to illustrate this: what is *narrow* by the standards of *shipping lanes* is likely to be *wide* (and indeed generally *big*) by the standards of swimming pools. Indeed, (4.6b) is a rhetorical exaggeration: the pool is clearly not going to be as wide even as a *narrow shipping lane*.

Adjectives of this kind are sometimes described as "relative intersective" adjectives. Unlike the "anti-intersective" examples, the denotation of an adjective–noun combination for relative adjectives is always a subset of the denotation of the noun alone: an *early Picasso* is definitely a kind of *Picasso*, whereas a *fake Picasso* is not and an *alleged Picasso* may or may not be. However, we cannot determine precisely what subset this is just by considering the denotation of the adjective: we have to consider the (perhaps rather idiosyncratic) way in which this particular adjective combines with this particular noun in each case.

In a further set of cases, it is unclear whether an adjective–noun combination should be interpreted in a fully intersective fashion or not. Consider (4.7).

(4.7)   She's a good politician.

We could use (4.7) to describe someone who is a skilled political operator, in which case *good* does not commit us to the view that this person is also a morally upstanding individual. Or we could use (4.7) to describe someone who is intrinsically *good* and who happens to be employed in politics. The latter interpretation is fully intersective: *good politician* in this sense denotes the intersection of "people who are good" and "people who are politicians". The former interpretation is only relatively intersective: *good* here contributes the meaning of 'good at the activity described by the noun that follows'.

In practice, we can sometimes exclude the possibility of fully intersective interpretations by appeal to common sense: if I describe something as a *good shovel*, you can assume that I'm not trying to ascribe moral qualities to an inanimate object, and for that reason I must mean that it's an effective implement for use in the act of shovelling. However, where ambiguities generally arise, we may need more sophisticated strategies than this for recovering the speaker's intended meaning.

Summary

This chapter introduced some additional features of adjective meaning. Gradability is characteristic of some adjectives, which may be related to their tendency to convey meanings along a single dimension; however, some adjectives are highly resistant to being used in this way, while others are marginal cases. We also saw that the modification of nouns by adjectives cannot be fully accounted for in terms of the intersection of sets denoted by the words. Indeed, we can identify different classes of adjectives according to the way they relate to the nouns they modify – and in some cases, a single adjective can modify its noun in multiple different ways. In practice, we are able to appeal to context to resolve some of the ambiguities that arise as a result of the nature of adjective meaning, a theme which will recur throughout this book.

Exercises

1. The adverb *quite* has two different meanings when it modifies adjectives. In one sense it is a "downtoner": *quite friendly* can be glossed as 'moderately friendly'. In another sense it is a "maximiser": *quite exceptional* is synonymous to 'exceptional to the fullest extent'. More specifically, *quite* is a downtoner with words such as *clever*, *late*, *small* and *unusual*, but a maximiser with *right*, *finished*, *impossible* and *alone*. What is the relevant difference in types of meaning between these classes of words?

2. Which of the following adjectives would normally yield biased questions if you inserted them into the frame "How [adjective] is/was X?", and which would normally yield unbiased questions?

old	young
rude	polite
unpalatable	tasty
weak	strong

3. Giving reasons, which of the following phrases would you say could be handled by an intersective account of modification?

royal visitor
royal correspondent
heavy eater
wise fool

4. Proxima Centauri is a small, cool, red star located near our solar system. In fact, it is the closest other star to the Sun. Comment on the meaning of the adjectives in the context of these two sentences.

Recommendations for reading

In addition to the general grammars of English mentioned in previous chapters, Kennedy (2012) provides a very readable discussion of adjective use and meaning, and some of its broader philosophical implications. There are many more complex papers on the semantics of gradable adjectives (for instance, McNally 2011), which get into some very interesting questions about the nature of the underlying "scale of measurement" for these adjectives, but these papers tend to assume a lot more prior knowledge.

5 Verbs

Overview

This chapter is about verb meanings. A simplified account of the semantic ingredients that make a clause, such as *Robby brought me the news*, is that a verb (in this case *brought*) "says something about" – that is, interrelates – the entities referred to by noun phrases (here *Robby, me* and *the news*). This is an oversimplification for several reasons – not least because verbs are not the only things that interrelate entities. Most of the meaning carried by the preposition *on* in *Those cups are on the shelf* could alternatively be carried by a verb, as in *The shelf supports those cups*; and the sentence *They made a fool of him*, containing the noun *fool*, has a paraphrase with a verb *They fooled him*. Nevertheless, there is enough truth in the idea to justify speaking about a clause as expressing a proposition by having a verb as its semantic centre and some accompanying referring expressions.

5.1 Verb types and arguments

Verbs differ in whether they require one, two or three noun phrases (italicised in examples (5.1) and (5.2)). As we shall see, this has systematic effects on meaning.

(5.1) a. *Billy* lies.   (i.e. 'Billy is untruthful'; one noun phrase)
       b. *Ella* admires *Beethoven*. (Two noun phrases)
       c. *I* offered *her a scone*.   (Three noun phrases)

In place of noun phrases, some verbs will accept preposition phrases in certain positions (for example, *to her* in (5.2a)). And sometimes positions are filled instead by embedded clauses, such as the *that*-clauses of (5.2c–e). A **clause** usually has a verb of its own and can carry a proposition: for example, *spring has come early* carries a proposition about the start of a season. In (5.2c) and (5.2e), this same clause is not free-standing, but has been **embedded** (that is to say, "packed into") another clause as the object of the verb *confirm*. In (5.2d) and (5.2e) we see a clause embedded in subject position. The word *that* is one of the markers made available by English grammar to mark a clause as embedded.

(5.2)   a.   *I* offered *a scone to her.*
        b.   *This evidence* confirms *my hunch.*
        c.   *It* confirms *that spring has come early.*
        d.   *That the daffodils are blooming* confirms *my hunch.*
        e.   *That the daffodils are blooming* confirms *that spring has come early.*
        f.   Offer *him a scone.*

The term **argument** is used to cover all kinds of obligatory, potentially referential constituents that verbs require, whether they are noun phrases (*this evidence*), preposition phrases (*to her*) or embedded clauses (*that the daffodils are blooming*). (5.2a) has three arguments. The main clauses in (5.2b–e) each have two arguments. (5.2f) has three arguments, because the "understood" subject 'you' counts as an argument.

A verb that requires both a subject argument and a direct object argument, such as *admires* in (5.1b), is called **transitive**. We could add an additional argument to (5.1a) – say, *Billy lies about his homework* – but the additional argument contains a preposition (*about*) and so this constituent does not count as a direct object. (5.1a) is therefore **intransitive**. Other verbs, such as *offer* in (5.1c), obligatorily require both a direct object and an indirect object: we cannot normally say **I offered her* or **I offered a scone* (unless the potential recipient is contextually obvious). (5.1c) is therefore **ditransitive**. It may also be useful to distinguish **copular** sentences, such as *John is my brother*, which tend to "predicate properties of a subject" (i.e. label the subject as having particular properties).

We can delve a bit further into the different categories of verbs. Intransitives have been divided into two rather opaquely named kinds (Trask 1993: 290–2) on the basis of the type of subject argument that the verbs require:

*   An **unergative** verb requires a subject that is consciously responsible for what happens. *Walk* is such a verb, and *Tourists walk through the eco park* is an unergative clause. A good test is acceptability with the adverb *carefully* because taking care is only a possibility when an action is carried out deliberately.
*   An **unaccusative** verb is an intransitive verb in which the subject is affected by the action but does not count as responsible for it. *Grow,*

Table 5.1 Examples of causative sentences with an entailment from each

Causatives	Entailments
The thought made her gleeful.	She was gleeful.
The children got the kite to fly.	The kite flew.
Bad weather forces us to cancel the picnic.	We are cancelling the picnic.
His inexperience is causing the decisions to go unactioned.	The decisions are going unactioned.
I had the students study this article.	The students studied this article.
The lock prevented him from opening the door.	He did not open the door.

drop and *die* are verbs of this kind. These verbs do not occur readily with adverbs such as *carefully*: **Mort carefully died*.

But we can also consider categories of verbs that have more elaborate entailment patterns than these, and we examine one important case of this in the following section.

5.2 Causative verbs

Because of the way meaning is constituted in language, it is not just a property of individual words but is also affected by the constructions they appear in (as foreshadowed in Section 2.2). This is strikingly true of verbs. For instance, the array of arguments in a clause can influence how the meaning of a verb is understood. If you encounter a usage such as *Robbers spray victims to sleep* (*Fiji Post*, 1 June 1995), you can readily understand that the intended sense is one in which *spray* is causative, because this is the only way to make sense of the fact that *spray* takes *to sleep* as an argument here. The intended meaning is that the robbers caused the victims to fall asleep by spraying something. The non-standard argument structure of this sentence indicates that the intended meaning of the verb *spray* is something other than the familiar meaning that would be appropriate for a headline such as *Robbers spray victims* or *Robbers spray victims with drug*.

The meaning expressed by a **causative** sentence is, in general, that a situation is brought about by whatever the subject noun phrase refers to, and the caused situation is described by the embedded clause.[1] Consequently, with causatives, the proposition carried by the embedded clause is entailed by the whole sentence. The sentences in the left-hand column of Table 5.1 are causatives and each one entails the sentence to its right.

The sentences on the right in Table 5.1 have either one or two arguments and they describe states or events. The causatives on the left share the following properties:

- They include a causative verb: in these examples, *make, get, force, cause, have, prevent. Prevent* is a negative causative.
- The subject (*the thought, the children, bad weather,* and so on) is an extra argument, in addition to the arguments of the corresponding sentence on the right.
- The subject of the causative sentence is used to refer to whatever entity – concrete or abstract – brings about the situation described by the sentence on the right.
- The causative has an embedded clause carrying the same proposition as the sentence to its right.

In each case, the sentence on the left affirms that the sentence on the right is brought about by some cause. For example, the person referred to as *I* caused the situation 'the students studied this article' to come about.

The verb in the main clause of a causative sentence is a **causative verb**. *Cause* is arguably a superordinate for the other causative verbs in Table 5.1. For example, *force* can be taken to mean 'cause an unwanted or resisted consequence', where the hyponym's meaning is (as in the cases of hyponymy discussed in Section 2.5) the meaning of the superordinate with a modifier. If we accept *cause* as the superordinate, we have the general entailment pattern shown in (5.3), where X is the referent of the subject of the causative sentence, and the single quotes enclose propositions (clause meanings).

(5.3)   'X cause ('clause')' $\Rightarrow$ 'clause'

Of course, the relevant details of the entailed clause need to stay the same on either side of the arrow: 'clause' is the same proposition both times. This is not entirely obvious in some cases because the wording changes. For instance, in *The children got the kite to fly*, the wording changes from *the kite to fly* in the causative sentence to *The kite flew* in the result. Unlike *The kite flew*, the clause *the kite to fly* does not encode past tense: however, we can think of it as receiving past tense from the main clause verb, *got*, which does encode that tense.

The embedded clause (the one in brackets in (5.3)) is an argument of the causative verb. Semantically, causative verbs have a minimum of two arguments, one denoting the causer and one denoting the caused state or event. We can call this latter argument the **embedded situation**. The embedded situation itself contains arguments. For the causative sentence *I made John give Mary the book*, the embedded situation *John gave Mary the book* has three arguments, *John, Mary* and *the book*.

5.2.1 More general causatives

Some sentences which lack embedded clauses appear nevertheless to entail causative constructions, and could therefore be seen as causative in their own right. Consider (5.4).

(5.4) a. The staff nurse gave Lucinda a key for the week.
       b. The staff nurse caused Lucinda to have a key for the week.
       c. Lucinda had a key for the week.

(5.4b) is a perfectly standard causative that fits the pattern described earlier, and does indeed seem to entail (5.4c). However, although (5.4a) does not fit this pattern, it also appears to entail (5.4c), in that (5.4a) entails (5.4b) and therefore also has all (5.4b)'s entailments. (The reverse is not true here: (5.4b) does not entail (5.4a). For instance, (5.4b) could describe a situation of **indirect causation**, for instance one in which the staff nurse lost a key and Lucinda found it. (5.4a) clearly seems to express **direct causation**.)

Tenny (2000) proposes that we can explain this by considering what *for the week* modifies in (5.4a). The sentence clearly wouldn't normally mean that the action of "giving Lucinda a key" lasted the whole week. In fact, a reasonable answer is that *for the week* modifies an "understood" embedded situation that is not made explicit in (5.4a), but which appears as an embedded clause in (5.4b) – that is, the situation in which *Lucinda has a key*. What (5.4a) normally means is that 'the staff nurse gave Lucinda a key, with the intention of causing Lucinda to have a key for a period of one week'. The *week* is semantically associated only with the situation of Lucinda having a key, not with the act of her being given a key.

If we think of certain sentences as containing "understood" embedded situations, we can find more sentences that follow the same semantic pattern as the more explicit causatives, but which do so in a syntactically different way. And there is some evidence for the existence of these "understood" embedded situations, from other aspects of language use. Imagine that a brand new bank starts offering credit card accounts with a low interest rate, and is subsequently obliged to raise that interest rate. Subsequently, its circumstances improve, and it is able to drop the rate back to its original level. In this scenario, that drop is the first time that the bank has ever lowered its interest rate. However, it appears to be acceptable to report that event with the sentence *The bank has lowered its interest rates again.* This use of *again* is called **restitutive**: it involves the restoration of a previously existing state (Tenny 2000). The acceptability of *again* in this kind of situation

Table 5.2 Three kinds of one-clause causative with an entailment from each

Causatives	Entailments
different verbs (e.g. *feed–eat*)	
She fed the baby some mashed banana.	The baby ate some mashed banana.
The bank has lowered its interest rate.	The bank's interest rate dropped.
Drought killed the lawn.	The lawn died.
morphologically related verbs and adjectives (e.g. *enrich–rich*)	
Nitrogen spills have enriched the soil here.	The soil is rich here.
The graphic artist enlarged the logo.	The logo became larger.
His job deafened Dougie.	Dougie became deaf (to an extent).
same verb form used causatively and non-causatively (e.g. *walk–walk*)	
The guide walks tourists through the eco park.	Tourists walk through the eco park.
The gardener grew several vines.	Several vines grew.
He broke one of his bones.	One of his bones broke.

is a reason for suspecting the existence of some kind of embedded proposition that is not syntactically visible: the *again* does not mean 'on a further occasion, the bank has lowered its interest rates', but something more like 'on a further occasion, the bank's interest rates are at their lower level'. Generally, where there is reversion to an earlier state, the adverb *again* can operate on the embedded situation, and this is evidence that the embedded situation is part of the meaning of the clause.

Let's look at some more examples. Recall that in Table 5.1 the causative sentences each had an overt embedded clause. In Table 5.2, the causative sentences are like (5.4a) in having only one clause syntactically, although for each of them there is an entailed proposition about a caused situation – an entailment that could be expressed by the corresponding sentence in the right-hand column of Table 5.2. In view of these entailments, it is reasonable to call the sentences in the left-hand column causative. And bearing in mind the relationships illustrated in (5.4a–c), the entailed propositions can be taken to be "understood" embedded situations in the causative sentences.

The last two lines of Table 5.2 show causatives entailing unaccusatives with the same verb form: *Gardeners grew vines* ⇒ *Vines grew*; *He broke a bone* ⇒ *A bone broke*. Fellbaum (2000: 54), who has done extensive studies of English vocabulary, argues that there are thousands of verbs of this kind: some common examples are given in (5.6).

(5.6)   *bend, dry, hang, hurt, lean, pop, spill, split, turn*

With the verbs in (5.6), this systematic semantic connection – causative-to-unaccusative entailment – is paralleled by a morphological link, in this case the fact that there is no change in morphological form between the two versions of the verb (also called **conversion** or **zero derivation**), as in *He spilt the coffee* ⇒ *The coffee spilt*. Regular patterns like this prompt the search for similar semantic relations even between unrelated word forms, as with *kill* and *die* in Table 5.2.

5.3 Thematic relations

Verbs differ not only in how many arguments they require, but also in how these arguments are related to the verb semantically. This is not just determined by the syntactic structure of the sentence. For instance, consider (5.5).

(5.5)   a.   John gave the book to Mary.
        b.   Mary was given the book by John.

Both versions of (5.5) describe the same action involving the same participants. However, they differ in the syntactic status of the noun phrases *John* and *Mary*. *John* is the subject and *Mary* is the object of (5.5a), while for (5.5b) the reverse is true. (This particular alternation, involving the passive construction, will be discussed in more detail in Section 10.2.3.)

   The term **thematic relation**, also called **thematic role** or **participant role**, is used to describe the role that a noun phrase plays in its sentence. Thinking in terms of thematic relations, we can try to understand the similarity between (5.5a) and (5.5b). In both cases, the relationship between *John* and the verb *give* is the same – the individual denoted by *John* is performing the action denoted by the verb *give*. Similarly, the relationship between *Mary* and *give* is the same in both cases – the individual denoted by *Mary* is at the other end of the action denoted by *give*, in that she is the recipient. And in both cases *the book* denotes the thing that is given.

   Of course, this is not only a property of the two sentences in (5.5), but a generalisation about sentences with the verb *give*: they require three arguments, one of which performs the action of 'giving', one of which 'receives' and one of which is 'given'. This is a more specific statement about the verb *give* than we made before, when we just said how many arguments it took. The fact that *give* takes three arguments is not an arbitrary fact about this particular verb, unconnected to its meaning

– rather, it is crucial to the meaning of *give* that sentences involving *give* have arguments that fulfil these vital semantic roles.

More generally, we can think of any verb as specifying some particular set of semantic roles that must be fulfilled by the noun phrases that complete the sentence. And we can try to group those semantic roles into coherent classes. In the case of *give*, we can label the required semantic roles as Agent, Recipient and Theme – this last term describing an entity that undergoes an action without changing its state. But other verbs typically require different semantic roles to be fulfilled; or, to put it another way, there are different ways in which noun phrases can be semantically related to the verb. For instance, we can distinguish cases such as (5.6a) from cases such as (5.6b), on the basis that the subject of the former is deliberately performing an action whereas the subject of the latter is not. We might call the subject of (5.6a) an Agent but use a different term, Stimulus, for the subject of (5.6b).

(5.6)   a.   Jane criticised Bill.
        b.   The onions made Bill cry.

We can also distinguish these from a sentence such as (5.7) in which the subject of the sentence does not perform or accomplish anything but is instead a recipient of some kind of input – in this case, we might call the subject an Experiencer.

(5.7)   Bill heard Jane speak.

In a similar vein, we can distinguish Recipients and Themes from other classes of things that are acted upon in some way. In (5.8), the object of the sentence undergoes an action and with it a change of state, unlike the *book* in (5.5) which remains unchanged: we could refer to *the car* in (5.8) as a Patient.

(5.8)   The tree damaged the car.

And we can also distinguish the Recipient role from the subtly different role of Beneficiary: in (5.9), *Valerie* is expressed as benefiting from an action without necessarily receiving anything.

(5.9)   David baked a cake for Valerie.

Numerous other semantic relations have been proposed, among them the (largely self-explanatory) Instrument, Location, Source and Goal. I won't attempt to catalogue all the proposed relations here. An important theoretical question is whether the set of possible semantic relations is small: if so, we could think of any verb as specifying that its arguments fulfil some of these particular relations. On the other hand, if there are verbs that introduce idiosyncratic or unique requirements for the semantic relations of their arguments, then the idea of semantic relations might not be very useful as a way of systematising the verb system of English. For instance, we could argue that sentences with the verb *hit* involve two semantic relations, "hitter" and "hittee", and that these are essentially unique to sentences with this specific verb. Although we might try to assimilate these each to a broader class of semantic relations, such as Agent and Patient respectively, it isn't entirely clear that that simplification would be valid.

Different approaches to grammar make different claims about the relation between semantic relations and syntax. One idea of this kind, due to Chomsky (1981), is the "theta-criterion": this claims there is a one-to-one correspondence between semantic relations (or their near-equivalent in the theoretical framework used in that paper, "theta-roles") and syntactic arguments, and that any sentence in which there is a mismatch between syntactic arguments and theta-roles will not be well formed. We could think of examples such as (5.10) as illustrating this idea, in practice: in (5.10a) there are not enough noun phrases to satisfy the requirement that *give* imposes for there to be an Agent, a Recipient and a Theme. In (5.10b), there are too many arguments for the verb *cry*, which only requires an Experiencer. And in (5.10c) there is no possible Agent, as required by the verb *request*, because both the noun phrases denote inanimate entities.

(5.10)   a.   *John gave to Mary.
         b.   *Bill cried Jane.
         c.   *The rock requested water.

Summary

In this chapter, we have considered the role of verbs within a sentence. It can make sense to think of the verb as requiring a certain number of arguments, depending upon its semantics, in order for the sentence containing it to be semantically complete. We can classify verbs according to how many arguments they require, but we can also identify specific categories of verbs that cause their containing sentences to give rise to specific patterns of entailment. And we can drill further down into the issue of how to complete a sentence containing a verb, by noting that many verbs – on account of their meaning – require their arguments to have specific semantic properties. We can think of this as the verb specifying a set of semantic relations that must be fulfilled by the surrounding noun phrases in order for the sentence to be complete. On this view, each verb is associated with a complex set of requirements that it imposes upon its containing sentence – and this property of verb meaning is associated with the traditional idea of the verb as the semantic core of the sentence.

Exercises

1. In February 2002 a UK government minister announced the resignation of a senior civil servant in his department. It was subsequently reported that the civil servant only found out about his own alleged resignation from listening to the radio. This led to a question in the media: *? Who is going to be resigned next?* In fact, the civil servant subsequently resigned three months later. Resigning is supposed to be a conscious act performed by the person who quits the post. If, in talking about the situation described above, someone had used the expression *? The minister resigned the civil servant*, would the sentence have been causative? Would it have the same meaning as *The minister made the civil servant resign?*

2. According to the nursery rhyme, after Humpty Dumpty's accident, 'All the king's horses / And all the king's men / Couldn't put Humpty together again'. Given that no one had put Humpty together on any previous occasion, what kind of verb is *put* in this sentence, and how does its meaning relate to that of *again?*

3. What is each of the following sentences: unaccusative or unergative? Give reasons for your answers.

   (a) *The kite flew.*
   (b) *My heart sank.*
   (c) *The students were reading.*

4. We could think of *pay* as a hyponym of *give*. How does the argument structure of *pay* relate to that of *give?* What is the difference in argument terms between *John paid Mary* and *John paid the bill?*

Recommendations for reading

Kearns (2011) and Huddleston and Pullum (2002) both offer illuminating accounts of the topics dealt with in this chapter. Lists of candidate semantic roles vary enormously between sources and between theories, an issue discussed by Croft (1991) and Dowty (1991). Dowty proposes to address this by positing more general Agent and Patient "proto-roles". Radford (2004) discusses Chomsky's theta-criterion with reference to syntactic theory.

Note

1. The sequence *her gleeful* in the sentence *The thought made her gleeful* is one that some linguists call a "small clause": that is, one that has a subject (in this case, *her*) but lacks any marking of tense. In this case, the sequence does not even contain a verb to carry tense marking. In Table 5.1 the clauses with *to*, such as *the kite to fly* in the sentence *The children got the kite to fly*, are infinitival clauses. Given that some linguists argue that you cannot have a clause without a tensed verb, the idea of infinitival clauses is somewhat controversial, and that of small clauses even more so.

6 Tense and aspect

Overview

This chapter is about two important aspects of how English grammar allows us to convey meanings. First, we consider how we can locate events in time, especially relative to the time of speaking or writing, which is the role of **tense**. Secondly, we consider how grammatical signals permit the sender to convey a notion of how an event is distributed in time: for instance, is it viewed as ongoing, or repeated, or compressed to a single moment? This is the role of **aspect**.

Example (6.1), from an article by Andrew O'Hagan, shows tense and aspect being used together to convey meaning.[1]

(6.1)   When I told people I was spending time with farmers, they'd say: how can you stand it, they just complain all day and they've always got their hand out.

Anyone who knows English can understand the essence of this sentence, but here we want to unpack something of what goes into understanding it. In doing so, we will explore the level of intricacy involved in communication about time, as mediated through the grammar of a language.

Let us imagine ourselves as hearers present at the initial utterance of (6.1). *Told* is the **past simple** form of the verb *tell*, so called because it is a past tense form and simple in aspect (that is to say, it does not involve any of the special aspectual meanings that are going to be introduced later on in this chapter). The past simple indicates that the event described in (6.1), in which the speaker 'told people that he was spending time with farmers', took place before the time at which (6.1) was uttered. Note that, although tense is marked on the verb, it is the whole event – or, more likely, series of events – described by the clause beginning *I told people* that is located prior to the time of utterance.

By contrast, *was spending* is in a form called **past progressive**. We can tell that this is a past form because of the tense marking on *was* (by

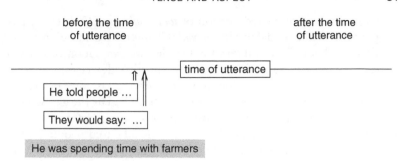

Figure 0.1 The main time relationships in Example (6.1)

contrast with *am*). When tense is marked in an English verb group such as this, it is marked on the first element in the sequence. **Progressive** aspect is marked by the combination of the auxiliary BE in front of the verb (which could surface as *be, am, is, are, was* or *were*, as appropriate) and the suffix *-ing* on the verb. Because *was spending* is a past form, we understand that the activity described by the words *I was spending time with farmers* was going on before the utterance of (6.1). Progressive aspect portrays an event as in progress during the relevant period of time, but leaves open the matter of whether and when it ended.

Figure 6.1 depicts the main time relationships in (6.1). Time is represented by the line running from left to right. The time of utterance is represented as an interval on the timeline, because it is to some extent elastic: the speaker can treat 'now' as being shrunk to a single point ('this instant') or as stretched to a longer duration ('today', 'this week', etc.)

The event marked by the past simple *told* is represented as occurring at a single point on the timeline because past simple forms encode events as if they could be located precisely in time. In this case, we might infer from (6.1) that the speaker is not talking about a single occurrence of talking to people, but rather a pattern of several occurrences, so we could instead point multiple arrows towards different locations on the timeline from the box containing the words 'He told people . . .'

The activity of the speaker spending time with farmers is shown as a grey bar located at least partially prior to the time of utterance, but not limited to a specific point in time, because that is what the past progressive conveys: the event was ongoing before the time of utterance but its beginning and end are not in focus. In this case, we also know that the event must have started before the event of 'telling people' took place, but we don't know that the event ended between then and the present day: it is quite possible that the speaker of (6.1) still spends time with farmers.

They'd say is a contracted version of *they would say. Would* is the past simple form of the modal auxiliary *will* (Chapter 7 has more on modal auxiliaries). There is no suffix in English that we can put on verbs as an indicator of futurity, so *will* is the main grammatical device for signalling future time in English. What does it mean to have a past form of a future marker? In this case, it means that the event described by the clause *they'd say* ... is a future event when considered from a past reference point. Relative to the time at which the speaker of (6.1) 'told people he was spending time with farmers', those people's actions are naturally in the future. However, relative to the time of the utterance of (6.1) itself, those actions are in the past.

In this example, just as we can think of *when I told people* as referring to a number of distinct events, so we can think of *they'd say* as referring to a number of distinct events. The first word in (6.1), *when*, links these two sets of events. Each of the actions of 'saying' can be supposed to correspond with an event in which the event of 'telling people' took place. Given what we know about how statements and responses are related to one another in conversation, we can pragmatically assume that the actions of 'saying' were responses offered directly to the speaker of (6.1) on the occasions on which he told people that he had been spending time with farmers.

The forms of the verb groups in the two clauses *how can you stand it, they just complain all day* are **present simple**. The time benchmark against which events are identified as past, present or future has now switched to the time at which the people said what they said about farmers. Present simple can signal different things, not just times coinciding with the time of utterance: it's clear that the actions described by present simple forms in (6.1) took place before the time of utterance of (6.1) itself, for instance. English does not have a grammatical marker of **habitual** aspect; however, the idea that an occurrence takes place habitually can be derived, in this case, pragmatically from the use of the present simple. By using *they just complain all day* to represent what the people said, O'Hagan indicates that he understood that they regarded complaining as habitual behaviour on the part of farmers.

The verb group *have ... got*, in *they've always got their hand out*, is in a form known as **present perfect**. It is present tense (we couldn't say **They've got their hand out an hour ago*, for instance). However, it is used to talk about the consequences of earlier events at the time of utterance. The people who spoke to O'Hagan were claiming that those who encounter farmers find them in the (metaphorical) condition of having a hand out, the farmers having previously got their hands (metaphorically) into that position.

Table 6.1 Two-part labels for tense–aspect combinations, with examples

	Past tense	*Present tense*	*Future tense*
simple aspect	**past simple** *saw*	**present simple** *see*	**future simple** *will see*
progressive aspect	**past progressive** *was/were seeing*	**present progressive** *am/is/are seeing*	**future progressive** *will be seeing*
perfect aspect	**past perfect** *had seen*	**present perfect** *have/has seen*	**future perfect** *will have seen*

6.1 Tense

The first element in the two-part labels indicates tense and the second indicates aspect. Nine different combinations of the two are set out in Table 6.1. This section will discuss tense in more detail, while Section 6.2 focuses on aspect.

6.1.1 Preliminaries

As discussed above, a given tense form can be used to convey various different time points or intervals, depending upon the time of utterance and upon other features of the sentence. Tense is a deictic feature of language. In fact, the process of understanding the temporal meaning of tense is more complicated than for other deictic expressions. For instance, an adverbial such as *yesterday, right now* or *in ten minutes' time* anchors an event in the past, present or future, respectively, relative to the time of utterance. In simple cases, past, present and future tense marking achieves the same effect. However, as the earlier examples in this section suggest, the mapping between tensed expressions and time periods is not always as straightforward as this: we sometimes need more elaborate pragmatic reasoning in order to determine the intended meaning of a tense form. As we shall see in the following section, the same is true of aspectual marking.

The forms that encode tense and aspect in English are the explicit markers listed below, although certain forms of tense and aspect can be indicated by default through the use of "unmarked" forms of verbs (*see, look, can,* and so on):

- Auxiliary verbs: WILL, HAVE, BE.
- Irregular forms of verbs: *saw, seen, thought, blew, blown, is, am,* etc.
- **Inflectional** suffixes:
  - past tense, usually written *-ed*

- present tense, usually written *-s* when the subject is singular, not the sender and not the addressee
- progressive *-ing*, for example in *am singing, was emerging*
- past participle *-(e)n* or *-ed*, for example *has seen, have helped*.

We'll now consider some of the time meanings that can be carried by these forms in practice.

6.1.2 *Present, past and future*

(6.2) shows some examples of the present tense being used with reference to events and states that occur or exist in a period of time that includes the time of utterance. We could tag *now* onto the end of any of these sentences.

(6.2)   a.   He goes for goal.   (Said by a sports commentator)
      b.   That dog is happy.
      c.   It's wagging its tail.

Present forms are also used for timeless truths, as in (6.3). Someone uttering one of these sentences is not just making a claim about what is the case at the time of utterance. The adverb *always* could be added to those utterances without changing the intended meaning.

(6.3)   a.   At sea level, water boils at 100°C.
      b.   Dark clouds have a silver lining.

While (6.3) extends the present tense to talk about timeless truths (which are admittedly also true at the present moment), the examples in (6.4) pair present tense forms *arrive* and *am* with adverbial markers of future time, *next year* and *next Wednesday*.

(6.4)   a.   You arrive in Australia next year in time for the Melbourne Cup.
      b.   Next Wednesday I am examining in Newcastle.

Both of these sentences are unproblematic – it's easy to imagine them being uttered in connection with a travel itinerary or a diary entry – and uncontroversially convey semantic futurity, despite the use of the present tense.[2]

Similarly, for the past tense, the examples in (6.5) demonstrate its basic usage in communicating about events and states located prior to the time of utterance. The adverbials *at 7 o'clock this morning* and *yesterday* similarly denote times prior to the utterance, and in this sense match with the tense forms used.

(6.5) a. We ate at 7 o'clock this morning.
     b. I heard it on the news yesterday.

However, the examples in (6.6) illustrate two well-known examples of divergence between the time of the event and the tense form used.

(6.6) a. They were watching TV when suddenly this truck crashes through their living room wall.
     b. If we introduced proportional representation, there would be more coalition governments.

The "historic present" form in (6.6a) is a way of describing a past event vividly by using a present tense form (*crashes* in this example). In (6.6b), the first clause is conditional, and puts forward a possibility rather than a past event, but nevertheless does so by using a past tense form (*introduced*). Possibilities are either in the future or not on the timeline at all.

Prediction is the characteristic function of the modal auxiliary verb *will*, as in (6.7a) and (6.7b).

(6.7) a. Lemon juice will remove that stain.
     b. A small rise in sea level and Kiribati will disappear under the Pacific.
     c. You'll get a chance during the coffee break tomorrow morning.
     d. He's going to stay at home and look after the kids.
     e. I am going to work.

Because predictions are forward-looking, *will* has come to be the nearest thing in English to a grammatical marker of future time, as in (6.7c). However, *will* is not the only way to mark futurity. We have already seen strategies in (6.4) that used present simple and present progressive forms for this purpose. (6.7d) illustrates another possibility, the use of *going to* + verb. Although *going to* can still convey physical motion to a place, it can also convey futurity, and in cases such as (6.7e) it is ambiguous between these two readings ('I am travelling to my place of work' or 'I will commence working').

A person who notices children playing by a river and fears that an accident is about to happen can say (6.8a) or (6.8b).

(6.8) a. Someone's going to fall into the water soon.
     b. Someone will fall into the water soon.
     c. ?Someone falls into the water soon.

These examples suggest that *going to* + verb is fine for any sort of prediction, just like the auxiliary *will* in (6.8b). However, (6.8c), using the

Table 6.2 The compatibility of some deictic adverbials with past, present and future time

Past time	Present time	Future time
then	*now*	*then*
last year	*at present*	*next year*
last Bastille Day	*nowadays*	*tomorrow*
yesterday		*in 45 minutes from now*
	today, this week, this year	

present simple *falls*, would be odd in this situation, although it would be usable if the event had been scheduled, for example if the action was part of a scripted dramatic scene. This is perhaps comparable to (6.4a), where the present simple is used to talk about a scheduled future event.

Not only is the future marked in a variety of ways, but – as we already saw in the case of *going to* – the markers used can have separate non-future interpretations. *Will* can also be used in at least one other way, for conveying timeless truths, just as the present simple was in (6.3). (6.9) illustrates this. It is reasonably clear that the speaker of (6.9a) is not making a prediction about an action that a particular diamond will be involved in in the future.

(6.9)   a.   A diamond will cut glass.
         b.   Water will always find its own level.

6.1.3 Tense and adverbials

Past, present and future time (relative to the time of utterance) can be expressed in sentences using various deictic adverbials, as we have already seen. Table 6.2 makes an attempt to systematise some of these relations.

The tense forms called present simple and present progressive can be used with adverbials such as *in 45 minutes from now*, as in (6.10a–c), but the resulting sentences present their events as taking place in the future, so that set of adverbials is shown only in the future time column of Table 6.2. A similar effect can be observed for the adverbials in the past time column, as seen in (6.10d), which achieves a similar narrative effect to (6.6a).

(6.10)   a.   Mark Lawson is here in 45 minutes. (Radio announcer describing next programme)
          b.   She lectures in Milton Keynes tomorrow.
          c.   He's visiting Scotland next year.
          d.   Last year, he loses his job.

Some deictic adverbials are compatible with all three times, as exemplified in Table 6.2 by *today*, *this week* and *this year*. This kind of adverbial motivates the description given for the basic present tense in Section 6.1.2, where we talked about events occurring in a period of time that includes the time of utterance. It cannot be just "at the time of utterance" because *today*, *this week* and *this year* denote periods too long to count as 'the time of utterance'. *Last year*, *next year* and the other items from the past-only and future-only columns of Table 6.2 exclude the time of utterance, but the versatile adverbials of the *today* set include not only the time of utterance but also times immediately before or immediately after the time of utterance (or both).

6.2 Aspect

Tense provides inflectional pointers to the location of events in time, relative to the time of utterance. Once you have "thought yourself into" the appropriate point in time, **aspect** comes into play. Aspect is about the grammatical resources for encoding the time profiles of states or events within an interval of time. By "time profiles", we mean the way that the event is perceived to play out in time: we can imagine an event as being compressed into an instant, or we can mentally stretch out an event and concern ourselves only with its middle stages, or we can concentrate on the culminations of events; and there are many other possibilities expressed grammatically in the languages of the world. Section 6.2.1 examines the distinction between habitual and "single-event" aspect. The two following subsections are then concerned with two kinds of aspect explicitly marked in the grammar of English: progressive (Section 6.2.2) and perfect (Section 6.2.3).

6.2.1 Habituality and simple aspect

The adverb *nowadays* triggers **habitual** interpretations of present tense clauses, as in (6.11).

(6.11)   a.   Maya loves music nowadays.
         b.   Tim drinks decaf nowadays.
         c.   Little Maurice brushes his teeth by himself nowadays.

It is clear that all these examples are about habitual matters: a single instance of any of the events described (for example, one instance of Tim drinking decaf) would not really license the corresponding utterance with *nowadays*.

Table 6.3 A range of sentences which all have habitual as a possible interpretation

Past simple	Present simple	Future simple
Maya loved music.	Maya loves music.	Maya will love music.
Tim drank decaf.	Tim drinks decaf.	Tim will drink decaf.
Little Maurice brushed his teeth by himself.	Little Maurice brushes his teeth by himself.	Little Maurice will brush his teeth by himself.

Habitual interpretations are available even without *nowadays*. Table 6.3 gives some examples which we'll discuss in turn.

The past tense sentence *Tim drank decaf* can clearly be a description of a single past event: for example, it could be used to tell us what Tim drank after dinner yesterday. However, it can also be interpreted as a statement about Tim's past coffee-drinking habits, under which interpretation it would mean the same as *Tim drank decaf in those days*, or *Tim used to drink decaf*. (*In those days* and *used to* are phrases that force habitual interpretations for past events, just as *nowadays* does for present events.) The same ambiguity applies for the other past simple sentences cited: each can be interpreted as habitual without explicit marking to that effect. All three sentences in the future column can also sustain a habitual interpretation: for instance, that – when he is a bit older – Maurice will regularly brush his teeth without help.

There is also a distinction between the first set of sentences and the other two sets. The sentences about Maya loving music denote **states**, rather than activities, a distinction discussed by Vendler (1957): if we say that *Maya loves music*, we are not talking about a single action in which she loved music, but rather about her general attitude of mind towards it. To put it another way, we are talking about Maya being in the condition of loving music, rather than performing a specific action or actions that involved loving music. Because of the nature of states, sentences of this kind – in past, present or future – have to be interpreted as habitual.

For the other sentences in Table 6.3, both the past and future forms can readily be interpreted as referring to single events – we could add *yesterday* or *tomorrow* to them quite easily – but this interpretation is not as readily available for the present simple forms of the sentences. The habitual reading is strongly preferred for these (Miller 2002: 148). To describe a single event happening before you, it would be more natural to say *Tim is drinking decaf* or *Little Maurice is brushing his teeth by himself*. Progressive aspect is the topic of Section 6.2.2 below.

To summarise: all of the simple aspect sentences in Table 6.3 allow a habitual interpretation, and this is the only interpretation available for the three state-denoting sentences in the top row. The other six are open to both habitual and single-event interpretations, but the habitual reading is preferred for present simple forms (although broadcast commentating, as in (6.2a), is an exception to this generalisation). Habitual interpretations can be made obligatory by the use of certain adverbials, but in the absence of these we have to rely on the context of the utterance (and the other material in the sentence) to understand which of the two possible interpretations is intended by the speaker.

6.2.2 Progressive aspect

Progressive aspect is marked in English by the use of the verb BE (in some appropriate form) and the suffix -*ing*. Semantically, it presents an event as an ongoing activity, drawn out in time, which we could think of as downplaying the start and end of the event and focusing on the middle phase. Particularly at the beginning of a narrative, the background to other events is often given in a clause with progressive aspect, as in (6.12), the first sentence of a novel by Michael Ondaatje.[3]

(6.12) When the team reached the site at five-thirty in the morning, one or two family members would be waiting for them.

In this example, the background is expressed by a progressive clause *would be waiting* . . .. Here, the 'waiting' is an ongoing vigil by family members at the site of a forensic exhumation. The forensic team's arrival is expressed through a past simple form (*reached*), thus portraying it as an event that occurs each day as a punctuation to the continuing vigil. This is, of course, assuming that (6.12) attracts a habitual reading: there is another reading in which the sentence makes a prediction about a single future event, but this is less accessible in this context.

Progressive aspect can be used to present even a short event as an ongoing activity, thus making it a possible setting for other events. For instance, (6.13) presents the departure of a bus as an ongoing activity, which the hearer is presumably being invited to interrupt with the action of boarding the bus.

(6.13) Hurry, the bus is leaving.

We can see that progressive aspect disregards the end of an event when we consider the entailments of sentences such as those in (6.14)–(6.16). These discuss events that can be analysed as "accomplishments" (in Vendler's (1957) schema). In each case, examples (a) and (b) entail that the goal was reached: in (6.14), that the building came down, in (6.15), that a napkin was folded and in (6.16), that a contract was drawn up. The corresponding sentences in past progressive form (c) systematically lack these entailments: they leave open the question of whether the event continued to completion.

(6.14)   a.   The firm demolished the building.
         b.   The firm has demolished the building.
         c.   The firm was demolishing the building.

(6.15)   a.   The waiter folded a napkin.
         b.   The waiter has folded a napkin.
         c.   The waiter was folding a napkin.

(6.16)   a.   They drew up a contract.
         b.   They have drawn up a contract.
         c.   They were drawing up a contract.

Many verbs that encode states resist the use of progressive aspect, as shown by the ill-formedness of (6.17a). When it is possible to use progressive aspect with such a verb, the effect is sometimes what Cruse (2011) calls "provisionality" – the idea that the state is currently in effect but may not be at some point in the future. This point is illustrated by comparing (6.17b) with (6.17c): there is a suggestion that the disposition of the keys in the former is less permanent than the disposition of the addressee's father's remains in the latter.

(6.17)   a.   *Who is knowing Danish?
         b.   Your keys are lying at the bottom of the swimming pool.
         c.   Full fathom five thy father lies.[4]

6.2.3 Perfect aspect

In English, the combination of the auxiliary verb HAVE and the past participle form of a verb marks what is called **perfect aspect**. The perfect (from the Latin *perfectum*, meaning completed) is used to describe occurrences in the **aftermath** of an event or state: that is to say, in the period (however long) during which the event or state seems to continue to have consequences.

For example, suppose we see someone grinning on her way back from getting exam results: we can see *She has passed*. The present perfect form *has passed* portrays the happy student not merely as being at a later time point than that at which she passed, but also as still being affected by passing, and hence still in the aftermath of that event. This is in line with the account that Quirk et al. (1985: 193) give for two common features of present perfect meaning: 'the relevant time zone leads up to the present' and 'the result of the action still obtains at the present time'.

Of course, if we signal that we are in something's aftermath, we signal that some event has been completed. Thus, the (b) examples of (6.14)–(6.16) convey that the relevant accomplishments have taken place. Consider the contrast between the examples in (6.18).

(6.18) a. The rain started.
        b. The rain has started.

Both (6.18a) and (6.18b) entail that there was a switch from 'not raining' to 'raining' at some point prior to the time of utterance. However, (6.18b) also normally conveys that we are in the aftermath of that switch: that is to say, that it is presently raining, and has been raining since the start that the sentence reports. By contrast, (6.18a) is consistent with a situation in which the rain started and stopped again (perhaps several times) prior to the time of utterance, and consequently doesn't commit the speaker to a view as to whether or not it is currently raining.

That said, what counts as the aftermath – and consequently, how we can interpret a sentence like (6.18b) – is somewhat open to negotiation. If (6.18b) was spoken by a scientist who predicted that climate change would bring rain to some previously arid desert, it could be used to report signs that rain had fallen there, rather than to report that it is presently raining there. This interpretation is habitual, so we see that the present perfect can be used to report a change (for instance) from something habitually not happening to habitually happening: the use of the present perfect here indicates that we are still in the period during which the thing is habitually happening.

Using the present perfect to depict a situation as being in the aftermath of an event can be a way of indicating that it has a bearing on the present. It would be odd to say something like (6.19) at the time of writing.

(6.19) ?Napoleon has gone to war with Russia.

Unless (6.19) is uttered by a character in a contemporary historical setting, it would be very strange to use the present perfect to describe an action which launched a conflict that ended over 200 years ago. Although historical consequences of this event may still be felt, it would be odd to claim that we are in the aftermath of it in the relevant sense. To put it another way, (6.19) would be acceptable if the outcome of the war mentioned were not already known, but given that it is, (6.19) is unacceptable.

Linguists have noted that present perfect forms tend not to accept past time adverbial modifiers, as illustrated in (6.20a). However, Klein

(1992) pointed out that the present perfect unexpectedly accepts members of a small class of past time adverbials, including *recently*. The contrast between (6.20b) and (6.20c) illustrates that *recently* behaves as a past time adverb, but (6.20d) shows that it fits with a present perfect. (6.20e) shows that the same is true for a preposition phrase with *since*.

(6.20)   a.   *I have arrived yesterday.
          b.   *They go there recently.
          c.   They went there recently.
          d.   They have been there recently.
          e.   They have been there since last week.

This pattern apparently arises because reference to the time of utterance is included in the meaning of these deictic expressions: *recently* means something like 'within a short period immediately prior to the time of utterance' and *since last week* means 'throughout the time period between last week and the time of utterance'. For this reason, they co-occur readily with present perfect forms.

6.2.4 Perfect aspect or tense?

Tense, rather than aspect, locates events in time. However, it must be admitted that perfect aspect does locate events relative to a time in their aftermath. From a present perfect like *The rain has started*, we can infer that the event happened before the time of utterance – even if only a moment before. That would appear to mean that present perfect is deictic. This is a reason why the perfect form is sometimes called the "perfect tense", as it is in Huddleston and Pullum's (2002) authoritative grammar of English.

Of course, in the present perfect form we also have a potential tense marker, namely the use of *have* rather than *had*. Using *had* instead would result in the sentences being **past perfect**, as in (6.21).

(6.21)   a.   When he phoned I had already sent the email.
          b.   When he phoned I had sent the email.

(6.21a) clearly places the telephone call in the aftermath of the sending of the email. In this case, the simple past (*phoned*) deictically points to a location in time before the time of utterance, and the past perfect *had sent* indicates a sending time before that. Even without the additional cue offered by *already*, (6.21b) can be understood in the same way.

For the classification of the perfect, it is potentially relevant to consider whether (6.21b) can also be used appropriately to describe certain situations in which the phoning and the sending of the email were simultaneous. On that interpretation, it would be equivalent to a past simple *When he phoned I sent the email,* which would make it a type of tense rather than an aspect. However, this question is still open (and well beyond introductory level): see Huddleston and Pullum (2002: 146) for more detailed discussion.

Summary

Tense is deictic. It locates events in relation to the time of utterance: past, present or future. In English, past forms usually appear with a suffix, present forms unmarked or with an *–s*, and future forms with various kinds of marking. Time adverbials also help to reveal the mapping between tense forms and time, which can be somewhat flexible in practice and difficult to pin down without appeal to contextual information.

Aspect is about the time profile of events. The grammatically marked forms in English are progressive (ongoing without attention to the ending) and perfect (we are in, or talking about a time in, the aftermath of the event). Habitual aspect is not grammatically marked in English, but is readily available as an interpretation for numerous classes of sentence, and is an essential interpretation to distinguish when attempting to make sense of tense and aspect.

Exercises

1. Table 6.2 presents various kinds of deictic adverbial showing the different times – relative to utterance time – that they are compatible with. Which group does *recently* belong in? And where does *soon* belong? You will need to make up sentences and scenarios for past, present and future tense and try them for compatibility with *recently* and *soon.*

2. With reference to aspect, discuss the difference in meaning between *Arthur's a tyrant* and *Arthur's being a tyrant.*

3. *A tobacco company told the Czech government that they had saved many millions of dollars because people were dying early.* Think of the sentence in italics as part of a newspaper report (and note that the pronoun *they* refers to the Czech government). Identify the combinations of tense and aspect used in the sentence and draw a diagram similar to Figure 6.1 to represent the relative timing of events, according to the utterance. That is to say, position 'time of report' on a timeline, then indicate the positions when the tobacco company told the Czech government something, when the government saved millions of dollars and when people died early.

4. Sentence (a) illustrates *BE to Verb* as a rather formal way of marking the future, such as a tutor might write on a handout. On the date mentioned, 11 May, the tutor could say (b) to remind the class about (a). Sentence (b) embeds a future tense within the past; *were* is a past tense form and *BE to Verb* is, as illustrated in (a), a way of marking future.

(a) On 11 May you are to submit a written solution to the exercise.
(b) You were to submit written solutions today.

Now try to find some less formal ways of embedding a future in the past. Suppose that you asked a friend yesterday to lend you a book, and they promised that they would, but they have now forgotten what they promised you. To remind them, you could use a 'future in the past' form: past because the promise was made yesterday, future because the book was to be brought at a time set in the future. Suggest one or two reasonable completions for (c) that involve a form of future marking with past tense on it.

(c) You said you _____ bring your copy of *One Day*.

Also, how might the request – corresponding to (a) – have been worded?

Recommendations for reading

Trask (1993) is a good first resort for looking up terms such as *tense*, *aspect*, *progressive* and *perfect* that may be unfamiliar. Chapter 13 of Miller (2002) is a short, clear introduction to the meanings associated with tense and aspect. Kearns's (2011) account of English tense and aspect is also highly accessible and systematic, and there are good discussions in Cruse (2011) and Saeed (2015). Worthwhile generalisations, as well as many interesting details, are available via the index entries for *tense* and *aspect* in Huddleston and Pullum (2002) and Quirk et al. (1985).

Notes

1. Andrew O'Hagan (2013), *The Atlantic Ocean: Reports from Britain and America*, Boston: Mariner, p. 163.
2. This is perhaps not so surprising given that Germanic languages tend to have two tenses, past and non-past (Hewson and Bubenik 1997: 209). The English present tense could be considered just as a non-past tense.
3. Michael Ondaatje (2000), *Anil's Ghost*, London: Bloomsbury, p. 1.
4. William Shakespeare, *The Tempest*, I, ii, 397.

7 Modality, scope and quantification

Overview

Modality is the term for a cluster of meanings centred on the notions of necessity and possibility: for instance, what must be the case, as in (7.1a), or what merely might be the case, as in (7.1b).

(7.1) a. This has to be a joke.
        b. The letter said the students might go there.

Expressions of modality in English (and many other languages) interact in an interesting way with other forms of meaning, notably including negation. For instance, (7.2a) and (7.2b) convey meanings that are at least very similar, suggesting that the expressions of modality *have to* and *must* are near-synonymous. But the corresponding negative sentences (7.2c) and (7.2d) differ sharply in meaning: the former is a prohibition, while the latter merely expresses that no action is required.

(7.2) a. You must report it.
        b. You have to report it.
        c. You mustn't report it.
        d. You don't have to report it.

The difference in meaning between (7.2c) and (7.2d) arises because, in (7.2c), the obligation encoded by *must* is understood to relate to the negative state of affairs 'not reporting it' (i.e. 'not reporting it is something you must do') whereas in (7.2d) it is the obligation that is negated rather than the state of affairs ('reporting it is not something you must do'). Differences of this kind can be understood as arising when different parts of sentences are affected by operations such as negation and the marking of modality: that is to say, when the operations take different **scope** relative to the rest of the sentence content. Scope is the second major topic of this chapter.

Scope is also highly relevant to the issue of quantification, which is the third major topic of the chapter. **Quantifiers** are words such as *all*, *some* and *most*. Like modals, these terms can also enter into various different scope relations with the rest of the sentence content, thus giving rise to different meanings. There is also a connection between quantification and modality, in the sense that what *must* be is expected under *all* circumstances, while events that are possible under *some* circumstances *may* happen, and so forth, but I shall not pursue this idea further in this chapter.

7.1 Modality

To put it very generally, a clause characterises a situation. Modality is the label given to the meanings signalled by the italicised expressions in (7.3). This family of meanings includes obligations to make a situation come about, as in (7.3a), and indications of whether the situation is permissible (7.3b) or feasible (7.3c). Importantly, it also includes a range of signals to convey how confident the speaker is regarding knowledge of the situation: whether, in the light of available information, it seems that the proposition is certainly (7.3d), probably (7.3e) or merely possibly (7.3f) true.

(7.3)   a.   You *must* apologise.
            b.   You *can* come in now.
            c.   She's not *able to* see you until Tuesday.
            d.   Acting like that, he *must* be a Martian.
            e.   With an Open sign on the door, there *ought to* be someone inside.
            f.   Martians *could* be green.

The main carriers of modality are a set of auxiliary verbs called **modals**: *will*, *would*, *can*, *could*, *may*, *might*, *shall*, *should*, *must* and *ought to*. However, modality is also encoded by various other expressions, such as *possibly*, *probably*, *have (got) to*, *need to* and *be able to*.

7.1.1 Modal verbs and tense

In Chapter 6, we saw that tense forms are not an entirely reliable indicator of time: it is possible to use present forms when narrating past events, and past forms for future events in conditional sentences, and so on. This lack of reliability is amplified in the case of modal verbs: as the examples in (7.4a–c) show, past forms of modal verbs can freely be used to discuss future events. These sentences have almost the same meaning as (7.4d), which uses a present tense form, although there is an intuition that the past tense forms (when used in requests, as in these examples) are somewhat more tentative and polite than their present tense counterparts.

(7.4) a. Would/Could you help me tomorrow?
       b. Might you be free to help me tomorrow?
       c. If you should have the time tomorrow, could you help me?
       d. Will/Can you help me tomorrow?

Having said that, past tense forms of the modals, particularly *would* and *could*, can be used for reference to past time, as in (7.5).

(7.5) a. Previously we would meet every New Year, but we don't now.
       b. Two years ago she could swim fifty lengths, but she can't now.

As pointed out in Chapter 6, although the modal *will* can signal futurity, it can also be used for predictions and timeless truths such as *A diamond will cut glass*. Marking of modality is in some respects complementary to tense marking: English syntax often forces us to choose whether a clause will have tense in it or modality instead. Biber et al. (1999: 456) analysed a corpus of text samples totalling 40 million words, from a range of genres, and found that modals were used in about 15 per cent of the clauses that could have them. The default pattern for English is for clauses to have tense marking but no marking for modality. (Exercise 1, at the end of the chapter, is about the relative strength of ordinary tensed clauses and ones that are modally marked.)

Expressions of modality exhibit an intriguing array of partially similar meanings. The modal auxiliaries are also among the most frequently used verbs in English: six of the top twenty verbs in English are *will*, *would*, *can*, *could*, *may* and *should*, each averaging more than 1,000 occurrences per million words of running text (Leech et al. 2001: 282). For both these reasons, modality is an important topic in English semantics and pragmatics. Whole books have been written about English modals and modality, for example Palmer (1990). The aim of this chapter is, naturally, more modest: it is to introduce a sample of the principal issues that make modality an interesting topic of study, some of the terminology used to discuss these issues and the crucial distinctions that are relevant to this area.

7.1.2 Deontic and epistemic modality

Two philosophical terms, epistemic and deontic, have regularly been used to label two main classes of modality. **Epistemic** interpretations have to do with knowledge and understanding. Markers of epistemic modality are understood to qualify the speaker's belief (or the belief of someone whose speech is reported) in the certainty of a proposition's truth. Modally unmarked sentences, such as the (a) examples in (7.6)–(7.9), offer us a baseline against which we can observe the effect of epistemic modality markers, as used in the corresponding (b) examples.

(7.6) a. The whole hillside is slipping down into the valley.
      b. The whole hillside could be slipping down into the valley.

(7.7) a. They meet in the final tomorrow.
      b. They may meet in the final tomorrow.

(7.8) a. Jessica went by motorbike.
      b. Jessica probably went by motorbike.

(7.9) a. The car was travelling very fast, so it came unstuck at the bend.
      b. The car must have been travelling very fast, because it came unstuck at the bend.

Modally unqualified sentences are found in cases where speakers have reliable information, for instance supported by their own eyewitness testimony, and when talking about events on fixed schedules. As illustrated by the modally qualified sentences above, modality comes in different strengths: (7.6b)–(7.9b) represent a gradient from weak to strong modality. Because of *could*, someone who produces (7.6b) is likely to be understood as conceding that the possibility of the hillside slipping down into the valley is not ruled out by the available evidence. The use of *may* in (7.7b) is likely to convey that a meeting between the players in question is compatible with some available information. The use of *probably* in (7.8b) signals not just that the speaker regards it as compatible with the available evidence that Jessica went by motorbike, but considers that the balance of evidence points to this having been the case. *Must* in (7.9b) is a marker of strong modality: a speaker who utters (7.9b) is vouching that all the available evidence leads to the conclusion that the car was going very fast.

Deontic interpretations of modality relate to constraints grounded in society such as duty, morality, laws and rules. Deontic modality allows speakers to express their attitudes (or relay the attitudes of others) about whether a proposition relates to an obligatory situation, a permissible one or something in between, as shown by the examples in (7.10).

(7.10) a. You can borrow my bike any time.
       b. The consul could have been more helpful.

    c.   You should email him.

    d.   Tax returns must be submitted by the end of September.

(7.10a) illustrates a common way of giving permission (although *may* is sometimes preferred prescriptively): using *can* (or *may*), the utterer offers no objection to the addressee borrowing the bike. In (7.10b), the use of *could* expresses the view that it would have been possible for the consul to be more helpful, and thus hints at the speaker's belief that it would have been preferable for the consul to be more helpful. *Should* makes (7.10c) a statement expressing what the speaker takes to be a desirable course of action. With *must*, (7.10d) conveys an obligation regarding tax returns.

As you may have anticipated, it turns out that the same expressions are often interpretable in two ways: as conveying either epistemic or deontic modality. The (a) examples in (7.11)–(7.17) are likely to be interpreted epistemically, with the modal expression (in italics) conveying the speaker's degree of certainty, whereas the (b) examples favour a deontic interpretation, with the modal expression conveying a meaning along the permission–obligation dimension.

(7.11)   a.   *Might* you have put the ticket in your jacket pocket?

           b.   *Might* I have another piece of cake?

(7.12)   a.   It *may* be dark by the time we've finished.

           b.   If you wish, you *may* copy these two diagrams.

(7.13)   a.   Random numbers *can* appear to have patterns in them.

           b.   The pigeons *can* have this bread.

(7.14)   a.   The tide *should* be going out by now.

           b.   You *should* try harder.

(7.15)   a.   The tide *ought to* be going out by now.

           b.   You *ought to* try harder.

(7.16)   a.   These later winters *must* be a consequence of climate change.

           b.   The treaty says that CO_2 emissions *must* be reduced.

(7.17)   a.   At 95 metres, this *has got to* be one of the tallest trees in the world.

           b.   He *has got to* be more careful or he'll break something.

The double meanings illustrated in these examples are more interesting than ordinary cases of lexical ambiguity: with modality, there is a sustained parallel. We could just list the different meanings associated with each of the lexical items, and thus observe that *may* can mean 'possibly' or 'permitted', *should* can mean 'likely' or 'desirable, according to normal rules of conduct', and so on. However, this would seem to miss the generalisation that each form reliably admits two interpretations, one epistemic and one deontic. A way of accounting for the related meanings is explored in Section 7.1.3 below.

Before we do so, it is worth underscoring the point that context influences the expression of modality. Given that the same forms can be used to express deontic or epistemic meanings, it is clear that we need some way to distinguish between these if we are to recover the speaker's intended meaning. Consider (7.18).

(7.18) a. Marie *expected the coffee to be strong*, she had ordered it before.
       b. Marie told the waiter that she *expected the coffee to be strong* and that she would send it back if it wasn't.

(7.18a) is epistemic, and offers a moderately strong expression of conviction on Marie's part about how reality will turn out; (7.18b) is deontic and offers a moderately strong demand about how Marie wants reality to be. The italicised material is the same in both cases, but coupled with reference to Marie's past experience (in (7.18a)) we naturally derive an interpretation under which it concerns certainty of knowledge, while coupled with a threatened sanction (in (7.18b)) we naturally derive an interpretation under which it conveys a reported demand. Note that in this case we have used a main verb, *expect*, rather than an auxiliary verb or an adverb, to emphasise the point that the epistemic–deontic ambiguity is fairly general.

In the absence of context, it is difficult to arrive at a stable interpretation of modal expressions of this kind. A celebrated related example was identified by the physicist Richard Feynman in his report to the Space Shuttle Challenger Inquiry, an investigation held into the catastrophic failure of that Shuttle in 1986. He argued that, given the available evidence, the probability of failure in one component, the Solid Rocket Booster, was likely to be around 1 in 50. However, he quoted NASA officials as arguing that 'since the Shuttle is a manned vehicle "the probability of mission success is necessarily very close to 1.0"' (Feynman 1999: 154). We could paraphrase this as (7.19).

(7.19) The Space Shuttle mission must be almost certain to be successful.

As Feynman pointed out, this has two possible interpretations: either that, given the available evidence, the mission was almost certain to succeed (epistemic) or that, given that the mission was manned, it was imperative to ensure that the mission was almost certain to succeed (deontic). Feynman, in effect, argued that NASA's statement was deontic, but was widely misinterpreted as epistemic, giving rise to a widespread public belief that the Shuttle was much safer than it actually was.

7.1.3 Core modal meanings

At the beginning of this chapter, modality was introduced as having to do with **necessity** and **possibility**. These notions are interlinked and interdefinable:

- What is necessarily true is not possibly false.
- Possible situations are ones that are not necessarily impossible.
- If it is impossible for something to be true, then it has to be untrue.

What does it mean to say that a proposition is necessarily true? An example would be the proposition that, whenever a whole number is multiplied by 2, the result is an even number. The way arithmetic has been set up, that proposition is always true: that is to say, it is necessarily true. However, modality is often used for communicating about matters that have not been systematised in the way that arithmetic has. In such cases, necessity is relative to the context as it is understood by the speaker and hearer. In ordinary communication, a speaker presents a proposition as necessarily true – something that *must* be the case – if it is the unavoidable consequence of everything that they assume to be true at the moment of speaking. Similarly, a proposition is necessarily false – something that *cannot* be the case – if its negation is the unavoidable consequence of everything that they assume to be true at the moment of speaking. And a proposition is regarded as possibly true if it is not necessarily false.

Of course, we may be – and frequently are – wrong about what is necessarily the case or necessarily not the case. Humans are not perfect computers that run through all imaginable scenarios: in everyday communication, we generally only take into account those aspects of reality that immediately strike us as relevant. Consider a logic puzzle such as sudoku. This is set up in such a way that there is only one possible solution, given the facts that are presented – but the details of the solution are not immediately obvious to us. The extent to which it's possible to point to a cell in the puzzle and say *This must be a 6* depends upon whether we can offer a logical argument that rules out all the other possibilities.

Epistemic modality gets used when the information that is available to us (whatever precisely this means, in practice) is not sufficient to establish the truth (or falsity) of the proposition being communicated. If we had enough information to be certain of the truth (or falsity) of the proposition, then we could express this directly without recourse to modality. Epistemic marking signals that the speaker is going beyond what is proven, one way or the other, and discussing propositions of indeterminate truth or falsity.

Have to is one of the ways of encoding necessity in English, and *may* is a way of encoding possibility. Revisiting two earlier examples, we can attempt to state the meanings of such sentences as in (7.20).

(7.20) a. *This has to be a joke.* 'Given all the information that I am able to take into account here, it is necessarily the case that 'this' is a joke.'

   b. *They may meet in the final tomorrow.* 'Given all the information that I am able to take into account here, it is not necessarily not the case that they will meet in the final tomorrow.'

Both of the examples in (7.20) can in principle be taken to be either epistemic or deontic, although in both cases the more natural interpretation is the epistemic one (in which *has to* and *may* both convey a sense of the speaker's confidence in the truth of the proposition expressed). Broadly, epistemic interpretations arise when the information that we are considering comprises facts about how the world is; deontic interpretations arise when this information incorporates preferences, wishes, requirements or recommendations. We could perhaps imagine (7.20b) being uttered by a wrestling promoter who is giving permission for the semi-finals of the tournament to be scripted in a particular way. The sentence could then be interpreted along the lines of 'Given all the information that I am able to take into account about what I want to be the case, it does not necessarily have to not be the case that they will meet in the final tomorrow'. Or, to put it more succinctly, the speaker could be interpreted as saying 'As far as I know, their meeting in the final tomorrow doesn't conflict with my wishes'.

This approach to the epistemic–deontic difference parallels what was suggested in Chapter 6 for the single-event versus habitual interpretations of simple aspect forms. In each case, the distinction is pragmatic: we can think of it as a context-dependent overlay on a semantic core that is indifferent to the distinction, or as a choice between two options that the semantic meaning makes available to us. The question of which factors cause us to decide one way or the other is a complex one: many things are likely to be at play. To take just one example, we might expect deontic sentences to have human subjects: it is, after all, people who are conscious of and guided by the preferences, wishes, advice and rules that constitute the foundations of deontic modality. For a similar reason, we might expect deontic sentences to contain activity verbs rather than state verbs: people's actions are arguably more amenable to influence through permissions and demands than are the states that they happen to be in.

Table 7.1 proposes core meanings for some important markers of modality in English.[1] To make it easier to focus on semantic similarities and differences between these markers, we can think of them each within the same relatively neutral sentence frame: for instance, *It___ be true*, considered as a response to *Is P true?*, where P denotes some proposition. For simplicity, we will only consider epistemic interpretations here: as before, if we were to consider deontic interpretations, we would need to think of preferences and requirements in addition to facts about the world.

By 'norms', we mean things such as schedules and averages, in the case of epistemic statements (see (7.21a) and (7.21b) for examples). In the case of deontic statements, we would have to understand 'norms' to mean conventions of conduct, as in (7.21c).

(7.21) a. There should be a train at 10.20, according to the timetable (but perhaps it's not running today).
        b. We shouldn't get snow in May, in a normal year (but exceptions do happen).
        c. The people who didn't cook should wash the dishes (but I'll let you off this time).

Should is a necessity modal, like *must*, but not as strong: exceptions to claims with *should* are coherent, as seen in the bracketed continuations

Table 7.1 Core semantics of some markers of modality in English

Marker of modality in the frame It ___ be true	*Meaning*
must *have to* *will*	P is true in all plausible scenarios, given established facts about the world
should *ought to*	P is true in all plausible scenarios, given established norms
may *might*	It is not the case that P is false in all plausible scenarios, given established facts about the world
can	It is not the case that P is false in any plausible scenarios, given established facts about the world

in (7.21), but attempting to do the same with *must* is problematic, as seen in (7.22).

(7.22)   a.   ?There must be a train at 10.20, but perhaps it's not running today.

        b.   ?The people who didn't cook must wash the dishes, but I'll let you off this time.

The meanings proposed in Table 7.1 make *must*, *have to* and *will* synonymous, and likewise for the pair *should* and *ought to*, and for the pair *may* and *might*. The table does not show various restrictions on use, notably the following:

- *Must* is hardly ever used for epistemic claims about the future; *will* is used instead.
- *Might* is generally weaker than *may*, perhaps because the use of past tense somehow serves to "distance" the possibility being discussed.
- Although *can't* clearly has both epistemic and deontic uses, *can* is sometimes unavailable for expressions of epistemic modality. For example, epistemic *can* is peculiar in the sentence frame discussed above: *?It can be true*.

Table 7.1 also makes *may* a superordinate for *can*. In permission sentences, *may* is generally substitutable for *can*, with some loss of precision but no major change in meaning, much as we would expect if *can* is its hyponym. However, this does not work in cases where *can* refers to an ability: *Can you help me?* is fine, but **May you help me?* is very odd. Similarly, *I can see for miles* is fine but **I may see for miles* is odd. On evidence such as this, some linguists propose to recognise a separate "ability" meaning of *can*, which encodes something called **dynamic modality**. The distinction is that the constraints encoded in dynamic modality originate inside the individual referred to by the subject noun phrase of the sentence. However, here we will consider dynamic modality to be a subspecies of epistemic modality.

7.2 Semantic scope

In Section 2.2, we discussed how words such as *unlockable* can systematically have two meanings, one in which the prefix *un-* combines with the word *lockable* to give the meaning 'not able to be locked', and one in which the suffix *-able* combines with the word *unlock* to give the meaning 'able to be unlocked'. We could describe these different derivational processes by using brackets, and distinguishing *(un(lockable))* from *((unlock)able)*.

Another way of looking at this is to appeal to the idea of **scope**: that is to say, the material that a particular **operator** applies to. We could think of the prefix *un-* and the suffix *-able* as operators on the meanings of other lexical items, which achieve the effects respectively of 'reversing the direction of change in a verb meaning' and 'turning a verb into an adjective of possibility'. Then we could say that the difference between *(un(lockable))* and *((unlock)able)* is that, in the former, *un-* takes scope over *-able*, while in the latter the reverse is true. So in the former case the resulting word meaning denies the possibility of something being locked, whereas in the latter case the resulting word meaning expresses the possibility of something being unlocked.

The general point here is that, when we have two operators in the same expression, we can get different meanings depending on which operator includes the other within its scope. This is an important issue for modality, because interesting things happen when modal operators interact with other operators, such as negation. Consider the deontic interpretations of the sentences in (7.23).

(7.23)   a.   You mustn't provide a receipt.
          b.   You don't have to provide a receipt.
          c.   You must provide a receipt.
          d.   You have to provide a receipt.

(7.23a) and (7.23b) are sharply different in meaning, but the corresponding affirmative sentences (7.23c) and (7.23d) are very similar to one another in meaning. How can the presence or absence of *n't* (and the auxiliary *do* that carries it in (7.23b)) make such a difference?

The difference between (7.23a) and (7.23b) is that the former conveys that it is necessary for a negative state of affairs to hold ('not providing a receipt' is obligatory), whereas the latter conveys that it is not necessary for a positive state of affairs to hold ('providing a receipt' is not obligatory). If we consider the operators here to be necessity and negation, we can think of (7.23a) as a sentence in which necessity takes scope over negation, while in (7.23b) negation takes scope over necessity. Thus, ultimately, (7.23a) is an affirmation of necessity while (7.23b) is a denial of necessity.

We can attempt to write these scope relations down using brackets, as shown in (7.24).

(7.24)   a.   necessarily (not (you provide a receipt))
          b.   not (necessarily (you provide a receipt))
          c.   necessarily (you provide a receipt)

Here, each operator is written to the left of a pair of brackets and the material inside the brackets represents the scope of the operator. (7.24a) reflects the relative scope of the operators in (7.23a), while (7.24b) does the same for (7.23b). Note that the components of (7.24a) and (7.24b) are the same: the only difference is in the relative scope of 'necessarily' and 'not'. (7.24c) represents the meaning of (7.23c) and (7.23d) in the same way.

Now, (7.25) gives examples of sentences with *must* and *have to* that seem naturally to give rise to epistemic interpretations: we can think of these as suggested explanations for why specific people have failed to turn up at an event.

(7.25)   a.   They must not have received the invitation.
         b.   They can't have received the invitation.

Traditionally, (7.25b) has been more popular than (7.25a) as a way to convey this particular kind of epistemic meaning in English, but (7.25a) has become more widespread (Miller 2002: 140), both with *must not* and with *mustn't*. The meaning conveyed can be schematised as (7.26).

(7.26)   necessarily (not (they received the invitation))

The idea that (7.25a) carries the meaning (7.26) is not surprising, in that it parallels the case of (7.23a) carrying the meaning (7.24a). However, in the light of that, it is surprising that (7.25b) also carries the meaning (7.26). There is an obvious difference between (7.25a) and (7.25b): one has *mustn't* while the other has *can't*. The two sentences are otherwise the same. *Must* and *can* are different in meaning (see Table 7.1), so we might expect *mustn't* and *can't* also to be different in meaning: but then, why do (7.25a) and (7.25b) not differ in meaning?

The explanation for this apparent paradox is that *can* generally falls within the scope of the negative operator attached to it in the words *can't* and *cannot*. (7.27a) is a reasonable paraphrase of (7.25b), whereas (7.27b) appears to express a different sentiment – a much less confident speculation.

(7.27)   a.   It is not possible that they received the invitation.
         b.   It is possible that they did not receive the invitation.

It seems to be a general rule about *can't*, or *cannot*, that its negation takes wide scope, while the negation attached to *mustn't*, or *must not*, does not. Exercises 4 and 5, at the end of the chapter, are on the relative scope of modality and negation.

An important general point about negation in English is that its semantic scope is not entirely predictable from syntax alone. We might expect that negation will take scope over a modal operator if the negation comes first in the sentence. As shown by cases such as *cannot*, this is an oversimplification. So we might instead speculate that the scope relations of operators have something to do with their relative positions in the syntactic tree. However, as we will see in the following section, a single sentence can have an unambiguous syntactic analysis but still give rise to multiple distinct possible semantic analyses. Additionally, there is a class of items – so-called neg-raising predicates (Horn 1989) – that cause negation to be interpreted in a way that doesn't accord with the syntax. For instance, the sentences in (7.28) appear to convey the meanings in (7.29) rather than the weaker ones in (7.30). It seems as though, in general, we are going to have to rely on combining information from several sources – lexical, syntactic and contextual – in order to recover the scope relations that the speaker intended.

(7.28) a.   I don't think Bill is going to win.
        b.   Elena doesn't seem happy.
        c.   Tom doesn't want to move to London.
        d.   Aliya doesn't intend to take that risk.

(7.29) a.   I think Bill is not going to win.
        b.   Elena seems unhappy.
        c.   Tom wants not to move to London.
        d.   Aliya intends not to take that risk.

(7.30) a.   It is not the case that I think Bill is going to win.
        b.   It is not the case that Elena seems to be happy.
        c.   It is not the case that Tom wants to move to London.
        d.   It is not the case that Aliya intends to take that risk.

7.3 Quantification

English provides a number of expressions that we can use to provide information about the number, or proportion, of individuals that have certain specific properties. These expressions include **quantifiers** such as *some, all, none, many* and *most*, as well as numbers, modified numerals such as *more than ten*, and so on.

We can think of quantified sentences such as those in (7.31) as making statements about the number of distinct entities in sets of things. In (7.31a), this is the set of cats that lack tails; in (7.31b), it is the set of men who have walked on the Moon; in (7.31c), it is the set of countries in Africa.

(7.31) a.   Some cats lack tails.
        b.   Twelve men have walked on the Moon.
        c.   There are more than fifty countries in Africa.

For this reason, before we discuss the meanings of quantifying expressions in general, it will be useful to introduce some ideas about sets as used in semantics and pragmatics.

7.3.1 Some basics about sets

A set is a collection of distinct objects, which can be of any kind. The objects in the set are referred to as the elements or members of the set. We can define a set either by listing all of its members or specifying the properties that its members must have in order to qualify as part of the set. (This latter option will be more relevant to our needs here.) A given element can be a member of multiple sets at the same time.

It is customary to denote sets by capital letters. If two sets A and B have exactly the same members, we can say that the sets are identical: we can write this as $A = B$. If every member that is an element of one set, C, is also an element of some other set, D, then we can say that C is a subset of D, and write this as $C \subseteq D$. For instance, if C is the set of numbers that are divisible by 9 and D is the set of numbers that are divisible by 3, every member of C is automatically a member of D, but the reverse is not true. We write the empty set – the set with no members – with the symbol $\varnothing$. (Technically we say that C is a "proper subset" of D if $C \subseteq D$, C is not equal to D, and C is not equal to $\varnothing$.)

We use the word **size** or **cardinality** to describe the number of distinct, non-identical members in a set. The empty set $\varnothing$ has cardinality zero. If $A = B$, both A and B have the same cardinality. We can write these relations as $|\varnothing| = 0$ and $|A| = |B|$.

We can combine sets in particular ways to form other sets. For instance, we can define the **union** of two sets, E and F, as the set comprising all the entities that are members of E or members of F (or both). We write this as $E \cup F$. We can define the **intersection** of two sets, E and F, as the set comprising all the entities that are both members of E and members of F. We write this as $E \cap F$. In both cases, it doesn't matter which order we consider the sets in: the resulting union and intersection will be the same. So it's true that $E \cup F = F \cup E$, and $E \cap F = F \cap E$.

Because of how these sets are defined, we can write down some statements about the cardinalities of unions and intersections relative to the cardinalities of the original sets:

- $|E \cup F| \leq |E| + |F|$. The biggest that the union of two sets can be is the cardinalities of those two sets added together. The union of the sets will only be this big if the sets don't overlap at all – that is, there is no single entity that is a member of both sets – in which case we say that the sets are **disjoint**. In that case, the intersection will be empty: $E \cap F = \emptyset$.

- $|E \cap F| < |E|$, $|E \cap F| < |F|$. The intersection of two sets can't be bigger than either of the sets individually (because it can only contain entities that are members of both sets).

We can also define the **complement** of a set as all the things that are not in the set. For the set G, we'll write the complement as G'. For any two sets G and H, the following relations will be true:

- $G = (G \cap H) \cup (G \cap H')$.
- $H = (H \cap G) \cup (H \cap G')$.

That is to say, we can divide any set G completely into two parts: the members of G that are also members of H, and the members of G that are not also members of H. This applies for any other set H. However, one of these parts may be empty: if G is a subset of H, then $G \cap H'$ is empty. If G and H are disjoint, then $G \cap H$ is empty.

This should represent all the theoretical machinery that we need in order to talk about quantifiers in terms of sets. It may seem rather abstruse, but hopefully the examples in the next section will help to make sense of it.

7.3.2 Simple quantifiers in terms of sets

Suppose we want to convey information about whether members of one set have a particular property: for instance, whether pandas are vegetarian. Depending on what we want to say, we might use one of the sentences in (7.32).

(7.32)　a.　*No* pandas are vegetarian.
　　　　　b.　*Some* pandas are vegetarian.
　　　　　c.　*All* pandas are vegetarian.

Let P denote the set of pandas and V denote the set of individuals that are vegetarian. (I'll just assume here that *vegetarian* can refer to any human or animal that does not eat meat.) We can think of the meanings of the sentences in (7.32) in terms of what they say about the relationship between the sets P and V. (7.32a) means that there are no members of P that are also members of V: to put it more formally, that the intersection of P and V is empty. (7.32c) means that every member of P is also a member of V: that is, that P is a subset of V, or equivalently that the intersection of P and V is equal to P. Figure 7.1 illustrates these two meanings in the form of Venn diagrams.

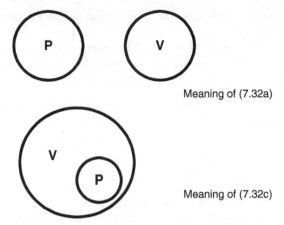

Meaning of (7.32a)

Meaning of (7.32c)

Figure 7.1 Venn diagrams for the meanings of (7.32a) and (7.32c)

(7.32b) is a little more controversial. Minimally, we could say that this sentence means that there exists a member of P that is also a member of V: that is, that the intersection of P and V is non-empty. However, if it were the case that exactly one panda was vegetarian, you might judge (7.32b) to be false on the grounds that 'one' is hardly 'some'. So we might instead say that (7.32b) means that there are multiple members of P that are also members of V: the intersection of P and V has cardinality at least two (or at least three). For convenience, I'm going to assume that *some* just requires the intersection of the sets to be non-empty. If that's the case, then we can write down analyses for the sentences in (7.32) in terms of sets, as shown in (7.33).

(7.33) a. $|P \cap V| = 0$
        b. $|P \cap V| \geq 1$
        c. $P \subseteq V$ (or $P \cap V = P$)

What if all pandas were vegetarian? In that case, (7.32c) would be true, but would (7.32b) also be true? According to the analysis above, it would, because $|P \cap V| \geq 1$ in this case. In practice, people are split on how they judge the truth of underinformative sentences like this. There is an intuition that *some* actually means *some but not all*, and if that's the case we would need to change the analysis above to specify this. However, there are good reasons to suppose that the core meaning of *some* is just as shown above, and that the meaning *some but not all* comes about by pragmatic enrichment. We'll see a possible explanation of why this happens in Section 8.2. Still another point of confusion is that *some* is not only a quantifier but also a word used in English as a plural indefinite article (as in *I ate some cakes* versus *I ate a cake*). However, here we're just going to be considering the quantificational sense of *some*.

We can provide a similar analysis for numerical quantifiers, as in the examples in (7.34). Rather than talking about pandas that are vegetarian – it seems odd to try to count the number of pandas in the world that are vegetarian – we'll discuss some examples concerning how many pandas are in the zoo.

(7.34)   a.   There are three pandas in the zoo.
        b.   There are more than three pandas in the zoo.
        c.   There are at most ten pandas in the zoo.

Let P denote the set of pandas and Z denote the set of animals in the zoo. A straightforward semantic analysis of the sentences in (7.34) might run along the lines shown in (7.35).

(7.35)   a. $|P \cap Z| = 3$
        b. $|P \cap Z| > 3$
        c. $|P \cap Z| \leq 10$

On this analysis, (7.34a) means that there are three distinct entities that are members of the set of pandas and that are also members of the set of zoo animals. (7.34b) means that there are more than three distinct entities that belong to both these sets, and (7.34c) means that there are ten or fewer distinct entities that belong to both these sets.

In practice, the meanings of numerical quantifiers in English are somewhat more complicated than this. Even plain, unmodified numerals, as used in (7.34a), are ambiguous: the sentence might mean that the number of pandas in the zoo is exactly equal to three (as in (7.35a)), or simply that there exist three pandas which have the property of being in the zoo, and that there may be more. And generally it's not at all clear that expressions such as *more than*, *at least*, *up to*, and many others actually have the meaning that we would expect them to, if we just appealed to mathematical intuitions about them. However, for the present purposes, we can assume that the analyses presented above are reasonably good approximations to the meanings of these linguistic expressions in English.

7.3.3 Proportional quantifiers

Most of the quantifiers discussed in the preceding section have a symmetry to their meaning. To say that *Some pandas are vegetarian* is equivalent, in terms of set membership, to saying that *Some vegetarian creatures are pandas.* Similarly, saying that *There are more than three pandas in the zoo* is equivalent to saying that *More than three of the things in the zoo are pandas.* This is simply because, for any sets A and B, A ∩ B = B ∩ A, which follows from the definition.

However, not all quantifiers possess this kind of symmetry. The notable exception in Section 7.3.2 is *all*: *All pandas are vegetarian* does not mean the same thing as *All vegetarians are pandas.* In terms of set membership, this is because the relationships C ⊆ D and D ⊆ C are not equivalent – in fact, the only time they can both be true at once is if C = D. So the only invertible sentences with *all* are ones in which the two sets being referred to have precisely the same members: *All even numbers are divisible by two*, for instance.

We could think of *all* as a special case of a larger class of items called **proportional quantifiers**, which express the proportions of sets that have particular properties. Some other examples are given in (7.36).

(7.36) a. *Most* pandas are vegetarian.
        b. *Less than 50 per cent* of pandas are vegetarian.
        c. *Few* pandas are vegetarian.

In terms of sets, we can think of these as making statements about the proportion of members of the set P that are also members of the set V. (7.36b) is perhaps the most clear-cut example: it appears to mean that less than 50 per cent of the members of P are also members of V. We can write that statement down in various ways. For instance, recall that everything is either a member of V or a member of its complement, V′, the set of entities that are not vegetarians. To say that less than 50 per cent of the members of P are members of V is to say that more than 50 per cent of the members of P are members of V′. This is equivalent to saying that there are more things in the intersection of P and V′ than there are in the intersection of P and V. So we can express the meaning of (7.36b) as (7.37), which we could gloss as 'the number of non-vegetarian pandas exceeds the number of vegetarian pandas'.

(7.37) $|P \cap V'| > |P \cap V|$

We could say something very similar for (7.36a): *most* seems to mean *more than half*, in which case we could write this meaning down as (7.38): 'the number of vegetarian pandas exceeds the number of non-vegetarian pandas'. In practice, there are reasons to think that the meaning of *most* is a bit more complicated than that: for instance, it seems to be odd to say something like ?*Most people are female*, but that statement is factually true if *most* simply means *more than 50 per cent of* (see Solt 2011).

(7.38) $|P \cap V| > |P \cap V'|$

Example (7.36c) is also tricky to define precisely. *Few* in this sense does not appear to refer to a stable number, or range of numbers: it appears to be context-dependent in that regard. The *few* of *Few people have been into space* is many orders of magnitude smaller than the *few* of *Few people voted in the European elections*. One way to characterise this might simply be to say that *few* requires the set of individuals with the property in question to be much smaller than the set of individuals without that property: that is, in (7.36c), that vegetarian pandas are greatly outnumbered by non-vegetarian pandas. We could write this down with the expression in (7.39), where << denotes the relation 'much less than'.

(7.39) $|P \cap V| << |P \cap V'|$

7.3.4 Distributivity and collectivity

Yet another distinction in the domain of quantification is illustrated by (7.40).

(7.40)   a.   All pandas are vegetarian.
         b.   Every panda is vegetarian.
         c.   Each panda is vegetarian.

These three sentences encode the same meaning, in terms of set membership, namely $P \subseteq V$. However, there is a sense in which they differ in meaning. Unlike *all*, *every* and *each* are **distributive** quantifiers: we can think of them as ranging over the members of a set and attributing a property (in this case, vegetarianism) to each of those members. By contrast, *all* appears to attribute that property to the totality of the set (of pandas) in one fell swoop. As a consequence, *all* can give rise to **collective** readings that are not possible with *each* and *every*. (7.41a) describes a different situation from (7.41b), and (7.41c) is acceptable where (7.41d) is not.

(7.41)   a.   All the students lifted a piano.
         b.   Each/every student lifted a piano.
         c.   All the students together lifted a piano.
         d.   *Each/?every student together lifted a piano.

In essence, certain sentences with *all* appear to be systematically ambiguous between readings in which they attribute properties (or accomplishments, etc.) to all the members of a set considered individually, and readings in which they attribute properties to all the members of a set considered collectively. This is a complex issue, when considered in detail, but I sketch it briefly here just to underscore the point that there is more to the meanings of some quantifiers than a straightforward set-theoretical treatment can easily capture.

7.3.5 Quantifier scope

Like modals (and negation), quantifiers can be considered as opera-tors with scope. In effect, they take scope over clauses, which express propositions; the quantifiers themselves are propositional operators. And as discussed earlier, the scope relations between operators can vary and give rise to differences in meaning. (7.42) presents examples involv-ing a quantifier and negation.

(7.42)   a.   All the books were not available.
         b.   Not all of the books were available.
         c.   Some of the books were not available.

(7.42a) and (7.42b) both involve the quantifier *all* and negation, expressed by *not*. In the case of (7.42b), there is no obvious ambiguity: the sentence seems clearly to mean that 'it is not the case that all of the books were available'. (This might also convey that 'some of the books were avail-able', but that can be explained as a pragmatic inference, as we shall see in Section 8.2.) By contrast, (7.42a) appears to admit two different interpretations. The first is that 'none of the books were available'; the second, that 'it is not the case that all of the books were available' (that is to say, the same interpretation as (7.42b)). The former seems to be easier to apprehend, when the sentence is presented out of context, but if you imagine (7.42a) as a response to *Were all the books available?*, the latter reading is achievable (particularly if the word *not* is slightly emphasised).

Similarly, although (7.42c) may initially appear to be unambiguous ('for some of the books, it is the case that they were not available'), it also admits a reading to the effect that 'it is not the case that some of the books were available' – that is to say, that none of the books were available. This reading is easier to obtain if you consider (7.42c) as the answer to the question *Were some of the books available?*

These pairs of readings are associated with different scope relations between the quantifier and the negation. The more obvious readings of (7.42a) and (7.42c) are those for which the quantifier takes scope over negation – we could paraphrase these respectively as *All of the books were unavailable* and *Some of the books were unavailable*. The less obvious read-ings are those in which the negation takes scope over the quantifier: *It is not the case that all/some of the books were available*.

Musolino et al. (2000) proposed a generalisation about sentences such as these, which they call the "observation of isomorphism". They argue that the preferred readings are those in which the semantic scope relations match the syntactic scope relations. In the cases above, the syntax suggests that the quantifiers should take scope over negation, and that corresponds to the semantic meaning that we obtain. However, it is curious that the "non-isomorphic" readings – those in which the semantic scope relations don't match the syntactic scope relations – are still available, and may even be preferred under certain contextual conditions (for instance, in response to the questions suggested above, and with stress on the *not*, neither of which changes the syntax of the sentence). A growing body of experimental work has looked into this issue, but as yet inconclusively. A cautious conclusion would be to say that hearers appear to take into account the syntax of the sentence, as well as the discourse context and any special features of the utterance, when disambiguating sentences of this kind.

Summary

Must, should, can and similar expressions encode modality. Markers of modality are interpreted either in relation to the demands and preferences of people, or in relation to evidence. With interpretations of the first, deontic, kind, *You must* ... communicates that the speaker demands something, *You can't* ... that the speaker disallows it, and so on. With interpretations of the second, epistemic, kind, *It must* ... conveys strong conviction about the likelihood of something being true, *It should* ... conveys that the proposition is expected to be true if things unfold in an average sort of way, and so on. Necessity and possibility are fundamental concepts, and relate to quantifiers such as *all* and *some*, inasmuch as what is necessarily true holds all of the time, and what holds some of the time is possible. Quantifier meaning can be expressed in terms of sets, using formalisms that were outlined in this chapter, and this way of looking at quantifiers elucidates the kinds of ambiguities that can arise from the sentences that contain them. In particular, sentences with multiple scope-bearing operators (such as quantifiers, negation and modal operators) can give rise to multiple interpretations as a result of the interactions between these operators. Understanding the speaker's intended meaning in such cases may involve integrating knowledge about the expressions themselves with information about the context of utterance, an idea that will be further explored in the coming chapters.

Exercises

1. There are differences in strength between modal verbs when they are used to indicate how certain a speaker is about a conclusion. What about using no modal verb at all – how strong is that? Consider the following situation: Edward has seen crowds streaming into a department store and says either *There might be a sale on* or *There's a sale on* or *There must be a sale on*. Rank these three in terms of how confident Edward seems that there is indeed a sale on in the store. Comment on what we can infer about speakers' knowledge of a situation as soon as they use a modal verb in talking about it.

2. Think about possible interpretations of the modality in the six sentences below. Can they be understood as deontic, epistemic, both or neither? Give a reason for each answer.

   They must be made from buckwheat.
   We must get up early tomorrow.
   The email needn't have been sent.
   I can hear you now.
   They might or might not make it.
   You better apologise.

3. Propose alternative scenarios for each of the following three sentences that could lead to their being interpreted (a) epistemically and (b) deontically.

   Guests may check in between 3pm and midnight.
   You must be a musician.
   He might say something.

4. In terms of relative scope, *can't P* means 'not (possibly P)', deontically as well as epistemically. The same holds for *cannot P*. What about *may not*? *They may not have an invitation* can be understood either deontically ('I forbid them having an invitation') or epistemically ('Perhaps they do not have an invitation'). What is the scope of negation relative to the scope of modality for these two interpretations?

5. I once heard the question asked on the radio "Which category of witness may | not be named in court?" As the vertical line indicates, there was a sharp intonational break after *may*. It was clear from the context that the question was about unusual circumstances in which a court would consent to certain witnesses having the protection of anonymity. For this meaning, what are the relative scopes of

modality and negation? To keep things simple, answer with respect to the sentence *The witness may | not be named.*

6. *In this part of the factory, one machine tests each product.* The underlined clause is ambiguous in terms of relative scope. State the two possible meanings clearly.

Recommendations for reading

Kearns (2011) provides good coverage of the topics addressed in this chapter. Huddleston and Pullum (2002) contains a substantial survey of modality, with many persuasive examples, along with a useful treatment of quantifiers. Van der Auwera and Plungian (1998) try to map out the ways in which the encoding of modality can and can't change in the history of a language: this might be an interesting paper to look at if you are studying Old English.

Note

1. The idea for *should* in Table 7.1 came from Papafragou (2000); *must*, *may* and *can* are loosely based on Groefsema's (1995) analysis.

8 Pragmatics

Overview

Up to now, this book has mainly focused on semantics – the abstract meanings of words and sentences, independent of context – although pragmatics was introduced in Chapter 1 and has been appealed to at various points since. In this chapter, however, we deal in more detail with the main concepts and principles of pragmatics.

Various proposals have been developed by linguists and philosophers for understanding how additional meanings arise when people put language to use in context, and for classifying those meanings. When we consider language in use, an important issue is how we do things with words: that is to say, how language enables us to perform social actions. That will be the topic of Chapter 11. In this chapter, we focus particularly on the question of how utterances in context give rise to additional propositional meanings that are not part of their semantics. Work in this area was pioneered in the mid-twentieth century by the philosopher H. Paul Grice, and has continued to be developed ever since. However, the focus of this chapter will be on the ideas themselves rather than their history.[1]

One of the basic ideas in pragmatics is that, as Levinson (2000: 29) puts it, 'inference is cheap, articulation expensive'. Language users save themselves effort – in speech, writing, typing, signing, texting or whatever medium – by producing utterances that deliberately rely on context to achieve their full communicative effect, safe in the knowledge that the recipient of the signal can use that context to infer information beyond what is made explicit. To illustrate this, consider (8.1), an exchange from a conversation in which A has told B that, on her trip overseas, she spent some time in hospital.

(8.1) A: I was bitten by something in Berlin Zoo.
       B: Was it an insect?
       A: Yes.

How did B guess that A might have been bitten by an insect? *Something* could denote pretty much any entity. Clearly B can rely on the semantics of A's sentence to infer that the *something* must have been an animate entity with mouth parts (although we can use *bite* metaphorically, so at a pinch A's assailant might have been some kind of mechanical apparatus). By the use of *something* rather than *someone*, we infer that A was probably bitten by an animal rather than an enraged zookeeper or a feral child. But, of all the animals present in the context of Berlin Zoo, why should B infer that the one that bit A was likely to be an insect?

Part of the reason seems to be that B relies upon implicature, a form of pragmatic reasoning identified by Grice. In Section 8.1 we will see how a relatively underinformative utterance, like A's first utterance in (8.1), systematically invites an inference that the speaker is not in a position to make a more precise statement: that is to say, A does not know what bit her. The starting point for this pragmatic inference is semantic: we draw this conclusion because of the meaning of *something* as contrasted with more precise alternatives. As we will see in Section 8.2, there are different ideas about how this kind of inference is drawn, and in particular the kind of assumptions that we have to make about the speaker's behaviour in order to arrive at conclusions like this.

An item of encyclopedic knowledge was also involved in the pragmatic interpretation of (8.1), namely that the animals on display in zoos are usually identified by signs. If A did not know what had bitten her, it was probably not one of the animals on display. The assumptions that speakers (and hearers) make about the knowledge states of the people they interact with are discussed in Section 8.3, on presuppositions. Another example is that, after A uses the expression *something* to talk about what bit her, the existence of this thing – the "biter" – can be treated as a piece of background information, presupposed by both speaker and hearer. This is part of the reason that the thing in question can then be successfully referred to as *it* by B. The kind of role that presupposition plays in connecting utterances to the previous discourse will be discussed in more detail in Chapter 10.

8.1 Implicature

One of the crucial insights in pragmatics is that we are able to infer additional content, going beyond what the speaker "literally" says, based on our knowledge about how communication usually works. Consider (8.2).

(8.2) A: Have you met Lucy's parents?
       B: I've met her mother.

Based on this interaction, A would be quite entitled to infer that B has not met Lucy's father. This is clearly not part of the semantic meaning of the sentence *I've met her mother* (or, to spell it out more fully, *B has met Lucy's mother*). It's easy to imagine that sentence being uttered in other contexts in which it wouldn't convey anything about whether or not B has met Lucy's father. Even in (8.2), the inference is potentially deniable: B might continue "I already knew her father".

What is special, then, about the context of (8.2) that suddenly causes B's utterance to convey this additional meaning? The essential point seems to be that we expect B to answer A's question. If B had met both of Lucy's parents, B could simply answer "yes". The fact that B does not do this, but instead offers a response that is less informative (and longer), can be taken to suggest that B is unwilling to answer "yes". And the obvious reason for B being unwilling to answer "yes" is that B knows that this would be false, and is of the view that it wouldn't be appropriate to make a false statement.

We can tell a similar story about (8.3).

(8.3)   A: Did you eat the biscuits?
        B: I ate some of the biscuits.

The case of *some* was touched upon in Section 7.3. There's a strong intuition that B is conveying that she ate some but not all of the biscuits, but in fact her utterance is quite compatible with a situation in which she ate some and in fact all of the biscuits. (I'm assuming here that *some* does not literally mean 'some but not all': there are good reasons for this assumption, but that discussion is a bit verbose for this book.) The intuition that B means to convey 'some but not all' appears to arise because we assume that, had she eaten all the biscuits, she would have said *all*. (Granted, B might be lying, but if she had decided to lie she could simply have said "No".)

The case of (8.3) is a little unlike (8.2) in that B's utterance in (8.3), considered on its own and out of context, would still seem to convey that B ate some but not all of the biscuits. The additional meaning, the implicature "not all", seems to arise almost automatically from the use of *some*. In (8.2) saying *her mother* implicated "not her father", but only in a context in which "(both) her parents" had been introduced as an alternative. *Some* seems to carry the alternative *all* around with it, which makes it a slightly different case.

Another different form of implicature is exhibited by (8.4).

(8.4)   A: Is Bill a good lecturer?
        B: He has an interesting beard.

In this case, A asks a question that seems to require a "yes" or "no" answer. B's response doesn't constitute a "yes", which might suggest that B actually means to convey that Bill is not a good lecturer. On the other hand, B's response doesn't constitute a "no" either, which might suggest that B actually means to convey that Bill is a good lecturer. However, the clear intuition about (8.4) is that B means to convey that Bill is not a good lecturer. The inference we draw here is slightly more indirect: by changing the subject, B seems to convey a reluctance to answer A's question. Given our collective attitude towards politeness in social settings, it seems rather more likely that B's reluctance is due to an inability truthfully to say anything positive about Bill's lecturing, rather than an inability truthfully to say anything negative about Bill's lecturing. Thus we conclude that B thinks Bill is not a good lecturer.

The first step in understanding B's utterance here is to realise that the apparent disconnect between that utterance and A's question is itself potentially meaningful, because we tend not to make irrelevant remarks in response to questions – at least, we don't do so if we're being cooperative. Once we realise that B is intending to convey more than is being explicitly said, we can use our knowledge about other social conventions to tease out the details of this intended meaning.

Still another example of pragmatic enrichment is evident in (8.5).

(8.5)   a.   This morning I got up, had breakfast and checked email.
        b.   This morning I checked email, had breakfast and got up.

Semantically (8.5a) and (8.5b) appear to be paraphrases of one another: both mean that the speaker performed the same three named actions on the morning of the day of utterance. Yet (8.5b) in particular seems very strongly to suggest that the sequence of events was a relatively unlikely one in which the speaker first checked email, then had breakfast, and only then got up. The explanation for this seems to be that we're basing our understanding of the utterance not only on what is said but on the order in which it is said – inferring in this case that the order in which the events were retold matches the order in which they took place. This in turn seems to reflect an expectation on our part, as hearers, that the speaker is likely to say things in some systematic order, and that in this case chronological order would have been a sensible one to choose.

8.2 The Gricean maxims

The process of inferring additional meanings, beyond what the speaker literally said, may conceivably have been around since the beginning of language, but attempts to systematise it are relatively recent. The most important development was perhaps Grice's (1975) proposal that pragmatic enrichments could be explained with reference to a set of communicative norms. Specifically, his proposal comprised an overarching Cooperative Principle which could be divided into four maxims, summarised below:

- **Quality**: Be truthful. Do not say things that are false or for which you lack adequate evidence.
- **Quantity**: Give the appropriate amount of information, not too little and not too much.
- **Manner**: Be clear, brief and orderly.
- **Relevance**: Make your contribution relevant to the current goals of the conversation participants.

A **maxim** is a pithy piece of widely applicable advice. However, Grice's maxims are not intended as advice about how we ought to conduct conversations, or rules about how we must do so. His claim was simply that communication proceeds as if speakers are generally guided by these maxims. In the following subsections, we'll revisit examples (8.2)–(8.5) and see how these, and many similar cases, can be explained with reference to Grice's maxims. In Section 8.3, we'll briefly discuss a more recent and influential account that treats these kinds of pragmatic enrichments in a somewhat different way.

8.2.1 Quantity implicatures

Equipped with the Gricean maxims, we can revisit (8.2), repeated below, and describe it more briefly as a case of an apparent violation of the quantity maxim. A's question invites a response in which B confirms that he has met both of Lucy's parents, but the information that B provides is less than this.

(8.2)   A: Have you met Lucy's parents?
        B: I've met her mother.

How can we explain B's utterance while still believing that B is a cooperative speaker, and therefore tends to adhere to Grice's maxims? In essence, we have to conclude that the obvious stronger statement ("Yes") is somehow unavailable. If B is obeying Grice's maxims, the only reason that "Yes" could be unavailable is if saying "Yes" would violate the maxim of quality – that a speaker must not make false statements or statements for which they lack evidence. Consequently, given the assumption that B is cooperative, we can take B's utterance in (8.2) to convey that to say "Yes" might be false – in other words, either that B hasn't met both of Lucy's parents or B doesn't know whether or not he has met both of Lucy's parents. In this case, it is reasonable to assume that B would know this: thus, we arrive at the conclusion that B hasn't met both of Lucy's parents.

In other cases, we might arrive at a weaker conclusion, because the speaker might not be knowledgeable. (8.6) is a potential example of this kind.

(8.6)   A: Is Rebecca in her office?
        B: Her car's in its usual space.

Here, B's utterance falls some way short of answering A's question – Rebecca's car could be in its usual space irrespective of whether or not Rebecca is presently in the office. However, we can reconcile that with the assumption that B is cooperative by inferring, just as in (8.2), that B is unable to make the stronger statement ("Yes"). In this case, unlike (8.2), it would not be as natural to assume that B is necessarily knowledgeable about the truth or falsity of that stronger alternative (that is, whether or not Rebecca actually is in her office), so we cannot draw the inference that that alternative is false. We have to stop at the weaker inference that B does not know for certain whether or not Rebecca is in her office – which is the inference that seems to arise naturally from B's utterance, given the assumption that B is trying to be helpful.

Inferences such as these are often called **quantity implicatures**, because they arise as a consequence of the maxim of quantity: more specifically, the part that notes that cooperative speakers give as much information as is necessary for the current discourse purpose. Schematically, they always involve an inference being drawn about a proposition that is more informative than the proposition expressed, and the inference is always that the speaker cannot commit to that stronger proposition, and hence either that the stronger proposition is false or the speaker does not know whether or not the stronger proposition is true.

In practice, quantity implicatures actually rely on the interplay between the maxim of quantity and the maxim of quality. A crucial step in deriving quantity implicatures from Grice's maxims is the inference that the stronger alternative would have violated the quality maxim, because it would have involved the speaker saying something that they knew to be false, or something for which they lacked adequate evidence. This only works because the quality maxim is part of the system, and the idea that we would sacrifice quantity in order to preserve quality rather suggests that the quality maxim is somehow privileged over the quantity maxim. That was certainly Grice's own view: he wrote that 'other maxims come into operation only on the assumption that this maxim of Quality is satisfied' (1975: 46). Adherence to quality is apparently the central plank of what is required to be a cooperative conversation participant.

8.2.2 Scalar implicatures

Example (8.3), repeated below, can be considered as an instance of a special case of a quantity implicature, called a **scalar implicature**.

(8.3)   A: Did you eat the biscuits?
         B: I ate some of the biscuits.

Presented in this context, B's utterance gives rise to a quantity implicature for just the same reason as (8.2): there was a stronger statement that B could have made (". . . all of the biscuits"). Assuming that B is cooperative, a plausible reason for their failure to make the stronger statement is that they are not sure that the stronger statement is true. Assuming further that B is knowledgeable, we can infer that the stronger statement is in fact false, and B did not eat all of the biscuits. Alternatively, if B is not knowledgeable (for instance, B does not know whether the biscuits eaten were in fact *all* of them), we derive the weaker inference that B does not know whether or not they ate all of the biscuits. All these inferences are cancellable without causing a sense of contradiction: it's OK for B in (8.3) to continue *in fact, all of them.*

As discussed earlier, the difference between this and (8.2) is that, for (8.3), the same reasoning holds largely irrespective of context, whereas in (8.2) (and (8.6)), the reasoning depends crucially on the context, because it is the context that furnishes the stronger proposition: if we take B's utterances out of context, they do not give rise to obvious pragmatic enrichments of this kind. In Gricean terms, *I've met her mother* and *Her car is in its usual space* are not intrinsically problematic with respect to the maxim of quantity: however, *I ate some of the biscuits* is.

A popular explanation for this is that the difference lies in the word *some* – and specifically that *some* enters into some kind of abstract relationship called a "scale" with the alternative *all*. The idea here is that the hearer who encounters *some* is disposed to consider the possibility that the speaker could have said *all* instead, and thus that the use of *some* triggers a classic quantity implicature. Consequently, the hearer interprets *some* as meaning 'some but not all' if the speaker is assumed to be knowledgeable about whether or not the corresponding statement with *all* would have been true. If the speaker is not assumed to be knowledgeable about this, the use of *some* gives rise to the alternative weaker implicature that the speaker is actually uncertain whether or not *all* is the case.

On this view, <some, all> is one example of an informational scale, but there are potentially many others, and these do not have to involve quantifiers: they can involve modal expressions, gradable adjectives or adverbs, or verbs. (8.7) presents some examples.

(8.7)   a.   It's possible that the team will win.
        b.   This coffee is warm.
        c.   Yvonne likes Ali.

In (8.7a), we can think of *possible* as entering into an informational scale with *certain*, and this sentence consequently conveying that 'it is possible but not certain that the team will win'. In (8.7b), *warm* forms a scale with the stronger adjective *hot*, thus causing the sentence to convey that 'this coffee is warm but not hot'. In (8.7c), *likes* forms a scale with *loves*, causing the sentence to convey that 'Yvonne likes but does not love Ali'. All these inferences are cancellable, and all of them depend upon the speaker being knowledgeable about the truth of the stronger proposition (which is very likely in (8.7b), where the speaker is expressing their own opinion, but not necessarily true in the other cases).

It is also a reliable feature of informational scales of this kind that they reverse in direction under negation: just as saying *all* is stronger than saying *some* in a positive sentence, denying that *all* is weaker than denying that *some*. Thus, we would correctly expect (8.8) to implicate that 'the speaker ate some of the biscuits' – because if the speaker hadn't even eaten *some* of the biscuits, they could have made a stronger negative statement than (8.8) with *none* or *not any*.

(8.8)   I didn't eat all of the biscuits.

In a similar spirit, the implicatures of (8.9) should reverse the directions of the corresponding implicatures of (8.7). And indeed the predicted pragmatic interpretations do seem to be available from these sentences: 'it's (merely) possible that the team will win', 'this coffee is (merely) warm' and 'Yvonne (merely) likes Ali'.

(8.9)   a.   It's not certain that the team will win.
        b.   This coffee isn't hot.
        c.   Yvonne doesn't love Ali.

8.2.3 Relevance implicatures

We can revisit (8.4), repeated below, and discuss it in terms of the maxim of relevance.

(8.4)   A: Is Bill a good lecturer?
        B: He has an interesting beard.

B's utterance here is, on the face of it, even worse than B's utterance in (8.6). While Rebecca's car being in its usual space is at least some kind of positive evidence for Rebecca being in her office, the interestingness of Bill's beard doesn't seem to constitute evidence one way or the other on the question of whether or not Bill is a good lecturer.

In terms of Grice's maxims, we can see B's utterance as a failure to adhere to relevance. However, we can still come up with some kind of explanation of B's utterance that explains this violation, without abandoning the assumption that B is a cooperative speaker. In this case, our intuition is that B has refrained from answering the question in a relevant fashion because none of the relevant answers are available to B. A possible explanation – perhaps the most likely in this case – is that Bill is in fact a bad lecturer, and B knows this. B cannot say "Yes" or "I don't know" to A's question, as to do so would violate the maxim of quality. B could, however, say "No" – and as argued earlier, the natural explanation for why B does not seems to be that it would be impolite to do so. However, this last point does not follow from Grice's maxims alone: we would also have to introduce some rules governing politeness (for instance, those set out by Leech 1983).

As we will see in Chapter 11, we have a strong expectation that – if the conversation participants are cooperative – questions will generally be followed by answers. Given an exchange such as (8.10), we will try to make sense of B's contribution as an answer to A's question, even if this involves positing additional background assumptions that we didn't previously know about (is it perhaps the case that B works early on Thursdays? Or that B knows the party is not tonight?)

(8.10)   A: Are you going to the party?
         B: It's Wednesday.

This tendency can also be seen as evidence of our preference for adhering to the maxim of relevance: we do expect that contributions to the conversation are going to be relevant to the current purpose or direction of that conversation. But in certain cases, such as (8.4), we cannot interpret an utterance in such a way as to see it as directly relevant. It is in those cases that we draw implicatures of the kind discussed in this section.

8.2.4 Manner implicatures

Finally, let's revisit (8.5), repeated below, and consider it with reference to the maxim of manner.

(8.5)   a.   This morning I got up, had breakfast and checked email.
         b.   This morning I checked email, had breakfast and got up.

As discussed earlier, (8.5b) rather strongly suggests that the events described happened in the same order in which they are presented in the sentence. We can naturally explain that inference as arising from the assumption that the speaker is obeying the maxim of manner, and in particular that they are being orderly. The speaker of (8.5b) has chosen to present the events in a specific order in their utterance, and it is reasonable to think that this might map to the order in which the events took place.

Having said that, there are other possible explanations for the choice of a particular order of presentation for these items. They could be placed in order of importance, for instance. They might be linked by some kind of causal relation. Consider (8.11).

(8.11)   a.   We sold our car and bought a tandem.
         b.   We bought a tandem and sold our car.

In these cases, we might infer that the event of selling the car preceded buying the tandem, in (8.11a), and vice versa in (8.11b). However, we can also read these sentences as expressing a richer causal relation: for instance, that the first action somehow served to make the second action possible. From (8.11a) we might infer that the tandem was intended as a replacement for the car, while in (8.11b) we might infer that the tandem turned out to render the car unnecessary. Again, these inferences are enabled by the presumption that the speaker is being orderly, inasmuch as causes tend to precede effects, so we might expect causes to be presented first (unless we explicitly mark the opposite relation with a word such as *because*).

Having said that, speech is necessarily linear: we can't say everything at once, so we have to choose an order in which to present multiple pieces of information, even if they are not linked by any temporal or causal relation. (8.12) is of this kind: the (a) and (b) versions appear to be essentially paraphrases of one another. In cases like this, we cannot derive much in the way of pragmatic enrichment by appeal to the maxim of manner.

(8.12)   a.   Her name is Moira and his name is Jon.
         b.   His name is Jon and her name is Moira.

The manner maxim makes reference to being brief, as well as being clear and orderly. Another subcategory of manner implicatures is related to this aspect of the manner maxim, as exemplified by (8.13).

(8.13)   Helen caused the car to stop.

Semantically (8.13) appears to be equivalent in meaning to *Helen stopped the car*. However, (8.13) expresses this idea in an unusually verbose and indirect way. By departing from the maxim of manner, the speaker seems to convey that something other than the usual sense of 'stopping the car' is intended: that is to say, (8.13) seems to suggest that Helen stopped the car by some other means than applying the brakes. As Levinson summarises it, 'What is said in an abnormal way indicates an abnormal situation' (2000: 136). However, like the other implicatures, the manner implicature that arises is cancellable – it would still be possible to say (8.13) if Helen was driving the car and braked it to a stop.

As with the quantity implicatures, manner implicatures of this kind rely on the idea that there was some alternative that the speaker could have uttered in place of their actual utterance, but chose not to. However, unlike quantity implicatures, manner implicatures do not convey the falsity of that alternative. Instead, they convey the fact that the meaning that the speaker intends to communicate is somehow different from the meaning that would normally be associated with that alternative.

8.3 Relevance Theory

In the previous section, we saw that we can systematise various kinds of implicature by considering the maxims that we rely upon in order to calculate the implicatures. The examples we considered encompassed all Grice's maxims (as well as politeness considerations). However, it's natural to wonder whether these four maxims represent the best way of characterising the relevant aspects of human conversational behaviour. As we discussed earlier, the maxim of quality seems to have a privileged status. It's also difficult to provide a precise definition of each of the maxims, particularly the relevance and manner maxims, in such a way as to avoid overlap between them.

Several later approaches to this issue have involved positing different sets of maxims: Horn (1984) and Levinson (2000) have detailed proposals of this kind. Perhaps the most radical account is that offered by Sperber and Wilson in 1986 (see Sperber and Wilson 1995). Their approach, **Relevance Theory (RT)**, takes the view that the whole system is most naturally explained in terms of relevance, a notion that they spell out in much more detail.

Specifically, Sperber and Wilson argue that, rather than relying on the existence of cooperative conventions in order to extract additional meaning from utterances, pragmatic enrichments come about because, as humans, we have a natural tendency to look for relevance in the stimuli we experience.[2] On their account, speakers are able to exploit this tendency in order to communicate more efficiently. We discussed a possible case of this earlier, with respect to (8.10), repeated below:

(8.10) A: Are you going to the party?
        B: It's Wednesday.

In this example, B can communicate additional meanings – beyond the fact that 'Today is Wednesday' – by virtue of the fact that A will try to interpret B's utterance as an answer to the question. The precise meanings will depend on context, and shared knowledge – one possibility is something to the effect 'I have a prior engagement (which you know about) and therefore can't go to the party'. The crucial point here is that if A did not proactively look for relevance in B's utterance, they might be forced to conclude that B had misheard or ignored the question, and the purpose of B's utterance with respect to that question would not be achieved.

Sperber and Wilson define relevance in terms of two components: cognitive effects and cognitive effort. A (positive) cognitive effect is anything that makes a positive difference to the hearer's representation of the world: for instance, knowing that a particular proposition is true. The utterances we hear – combined with our background knowledge – are a potential source of cognitive effects, in that we can use the information in them to learn new things about the world. Cognitive effort refers to the amount of mental resources, such as memory and inferential processing, that we use in order to obtain cognitive effects. All things being equal, a stimulus (such as an utterance) is more relevant than another if it gives rise to greater cognitive effects; and it is more relevant if it requires less cognitive effort to process.

The central claim of Relevance Theory is that human cognition has evolved in such a way as to maximise relevance, in terms of how we process linguistic inputs. As Wilson and Sperber (2002: 254) put it, "our perceptual mechanisms tend automatically to pick out potentially relevant stimuli, our memory retrieval mechanisms tend automatically to activate potentially relevant assumptions, and our inferential mechanisms tend spontaneously to process them in the most productive way". Coupled to this principle, RT posits a second principle that applies to linguistic communication (and certain other forms of communication), namely that every utterance conveys, in addition to its meaning, the fact of its own relevance. Thus, when we hear an utterance, we are entitled to assume that it is worth our while to process it, and also that it is the best the speaker could do, in terms of maximising relevance.

Equipped with this notion of relevance, we can offer an alternative explanation for the implicatures related to the Gricean maxims of quantity and manner, as well as those arising from Gricean relevance considerations. Let's turn once more to (8.2).

(8.2)   A: Have you met Lucy's parents?
          B: I've met her mother.

In RT terms, it would have been more relevant for B to say "yes", if that had been true: that way, A would have access to more information (greater cognitive effects) and would have had to process a simpler stimulus (less cognitive effort). Assuming that B is attempting to maximise relevance, we're forced to conclude that it wouldn't have been true to say "yes".

A similar argument applies to (8.13), repeated below.

(8.13)   Helen caused the car to stop.

Again, we can make the case that it would have been more relevant for the speaker to say "Helen stopped the car": that would have involved less effort on the part of the hearer. Consequently, to explain why the speaker did not do this, we are obliged to assume that the speaker intended to convey some additional meaning that would not normally be available to someone who heard "Helen stopped the car". Given our background knowledge about how one would normally stop a car, the inference emerges from (8.13) that Helen caused the car to stop in some other way than pressing the brake pedal.

Relevance Theory offers a very useful way to characterise certain inferences, and offers an interesting perspective on how we perform pragmatic inference in general. However, as an approach, it has its limitations. There is no consensus about how to quantify cognitive effects or cognitive effort, so in practice we can't simply take utterances and evaluate their relevance according to some scale. Rather, as observed by Wilson and Sperber (2002: 253), we can compare pairs of alternatives and argue that one is more relevant than the other. They argue that this is, in any case, more psychologically plausible than a fully quantitative approach in which we consider the absolute relevance of any given utterance. On the other hand, without a clear way of measuring cognitive effects or cognitive effort, it is very difficult to disprove any claim couched in terms of relevance: if we draw an inference from a particular utterance, we can say that the effects must have justified the effort, and if we don't draw an inference from that utterance, we can say that the effects must not have justified the effort. In such cases, RT doesn't very clearly predict whether or not a particular pragmatic enrichment is going to be available.

8.4 Presuppositions

When we communicate, we take certain background assumptions for granted: we can rely upon our hearer already knowing things about the nature of language (for instance, the meanings of words), but also about the existence of certain entities, the fact of certain events having taken place, and so on. **Presupposition** is the term for a particular kind of inference that concerns these assumptions. Inferences in this class are an important way for speakers to give hints, during the process of utterance, about the assumptions that they are currently taking for granted.

Perhaps the most widespread example of presupposition in language is the so-called "existential" presupposition that is carried by noun phrases. When we use a noun phrase, we presuppose that this has reference. Consider (8.14).

(8.14)   a.   Julia worked as a photojournalist in Iraq during the war.
         b.   Julia worked as a photojournalist in Switzerland during the war.
         c.   Julia worked as a photojournalist in Mali during the war.

In (8.14a), the speaker presupposes the existence of someone named Julia, something called a photojournalist, something called Iraq and something called the war. Assuming that it's common knowledge between speaker and hearer that there have been wars in Iraq, we would naturally interpret *the war* as referring to one of those wars. If one of the entities referred to did not exist, we would not be able to interpret the utterance as making a meaningful statement about the world. In (8.14b), we might assume that it is common knowledge that there have been no wars in Switzerland (at least none that were contemporary with the existence of the profession of photojournalism). We might interpret *the war* to mean a particularly salient war, such as World War II: but if that is not a sensible option, for instance because Julia was born in 1970, we might be tempted to reply "What war?" In doing so, we would be challenging one of the existential presuppositions of the sentence.

The third option, (8.14c), represents an interesting case: it might not be common knowledge that there has been a recent war in Mali, so the hearer of (8.14c) might effectively learn this from the utterance, even though the speaker is acting as though this is already common knowledge. In a case like this, we say that the presupposition is **accommodated**: the hearer adds it to their knowledge base and the interaction proceeds as though the presupposition had been common ground all along.

Although numerous, and useful, existential presuppositions are perhaps not very interesting: they generally amount to the presupposition that a referring expression actually has reference. Some diverting philosophical questions arise about how to handle expressions that have no reference in the real world, such as *unicorn*, but these issues are not crucial for us here. However, in addition to noun phrases introducing existential presuppositions, the English language provides us with many linguistic devices for signalling the existence of presuppositions of many diverse kinds.

If, having missed out on the first distribution of dessert, you are asked "Would you like some more?", you cannot really answer with a simple "Yes, please" or "No, thank you". *More* presupposes that you have already had some. This presupposition arises whether *more* is used in the context of this kind of question or in the corresponding assertion "I would like some more", which is why "Yes" (which conveys this assertion) is inappropriate here. The reason that the response "No, thank you" is inappropriate is that the presupposition persists here: we could interpret this as being a polite way of saying "I won't have any more", which continues to presuppose that the speaker has already had some dessert. So *more* is still in there, still pointing to the same false presupposition that you have already had some dessert.

What is presupposed is, by its nature, background information. It is not asserted, so it does not count as the overtly presented information carried by an utterance. Presuppositions are triggered by particular words (and syntactic patterns), and in that respect they are akin to the encoded-in-the-language meanings that characterise semantics. However, they do exhibit important differences, as illustrated by (8.15)–(8.17).

(8.15) a. Hana forgot to post the letter
        b. Hana did not forget to post the letter.
        c. Did Hana forget to post the letter?
        d. Hana was supposed to post the letter.

(8.16) a. Dick has started smoking.
        b. Dick hasn't started smoking.
        c. Has Dick started smoking?
        d. Dick did not previously smoke.

(8.17) a. The treatment has cured her uncle.
        b. The treatment hasn't cured her uncle.
        c. Has the treatment cured her uncle?
        d. Her uncle was ill.

In each of these sets, the (a), (b) and (c) sentences presuppose the corresponding (d) sentence: the triggers for the presuppositions are the verbs *forget, start* and *cure*. These examples highlight a distinguishing feature of presuppositions: they are not affected by the negation of the asserted part of the sentence, and questioning the main part of the sentence also leaves the presuppositions intact. This is related to the fact that presuppositions are information that is assumed to be true. By way of contrast, (8.18) shows that entailments do not generally survive negation: (8.18a) entails (8.18c), but (8.18b) does not entail (8.18c).

(8.18) a. The treatment has cured her uncle.
        b. The treatment hasn't cured her uncle.
        c. Her uncle is now well.

Presuppositions are different from entailments in another important respect: they can be cancelled, as illustrated in (8.19). This has been taken as evidence that they are essentially pragmatic rather than semantic in nature. When presuppositions are cancelled in this way, there is a danger of communication being derailed, and a warning to that effect can be signalled by emphasis on the stressed syllable of the presupposition trigger (for instance, the *get* of *forget*).

(8.19) a. Hana didn't forget to post the letter; she didn't know it needed to go.
        b. Dick hasn't started smoking; he's been smoking for years.
        c. The treatment hasn't cured her uncle; he wasn't ill in the first place.

The above examples are just a small sample of the full set of presupposition triggers in English. In addition to *start*, we have items such as *begin, commence, stop, pause* and many others besides. Restitutive *again*, discussed in Section 5.2.1, triggers a presupposition about a state or activity having existed before. The quantifier *both* presupposes that just two entities are being spoken about; and so on.

There is also a class of items, often called **factives**, that have been extensively studied as presupposition triggers (see Huddleston and Pullum 2002: 1004–11). These include verbs such as *regret, matter, realise* and *explain*, and adjectives which combine with the verb BE, such as *odd, sorry, aware*, and so on. They can be used to introduce a clause that the speaker, in normal circumstances, presumes to be true. A sample of factive sentences is given in (8.20)–(8.22): again, in each case, (a), (b) and (c) all presuppose (d).

(8.20) a. It matters that they lied to us.
        b. It doesn't matter that they lied to us.

      c.   Does it matter that they lied to us?
      d.   They lied to us.

(8.21)   a.   Jill explained that the train was late.
      b.   Jill didn't explain that the train was late.
      c.   Did Jill explain that the train was late?
      d.   The train was late.

(8.22)   a.   Rob is sorry that the World Cup is over.
      b.   Rob is not sorry that the World Cup is over.
      c.   Is Rob sorry that the World Cup is over?
      d.   The World Cup is over.

For comparison, the sentences in (8.23) use a non-factive verb, *prove*.

(8.23)   a.   This proves that they lied to us.
      b.   This doesn't prove that they lied to us.
      c.   Does this prove that they lied to us?
      d.   They lied to us.

With *prove*, (8.23a) entails (8.23d), but – as expected for an entail-ment – this is no longer the case when the sentence is negated, or when the content is expressed in the form of a question. Neither (8.23b) nor (8.23c) entails (8.23d). For this reason, this inference does not count as a presupposition.

Earlier I alluded to the fact that syntactic constructions can also trigger presuppositions. Relative clauses exemplify this: in (8.24), the clause *that Admin sent us* gives rise to a presupposition. (In this case, it is essentially an existential presupposition concerning the existence of "an email that Admin sent us".) Again, the (a), (b) and (c) sentences each presuppose the (d) sentence.

(8.24)   a.   The email that Admin sent us said Thursday.
      b.   It's not true that the email that Admin sent us said Thursday.
      c.   Did the email that Admin sent us say Thursday?
      d.   Admin sent us an email.

Time clauses with past reference also trigger presuppositions. (8.25a) presupposes (8.25b). If the situation described by (8.25b) never took place, then the use of (8.25a) is likely to lead to, at best, puzzlement.

(8.25)   a.   I loved you when we were in Monterrey.
      b.   We were in Monterrey.

Finally, let's briefly consider the status of presupposed information. Does it count as having been communicated? In cases where the presupposition is genuinely common knowledge between speaker and hearer at the time of utterance, this is a bit of a moot point: whether or not the presupposition is communicated, both the speaker and the hearer already know it and continue to know it. But, as discussed with reference to (8.14c) – repeated below – utterances carrying presuppositions can be made in certain circumstances even when the presupposition is not already known to the hearer.

(8.14)   c.   Julia worked as a photojournalist in Mali during the war.

Hearers tend to show some willingness to accommodate presuppositions – that is, to add them to their own stock of knowledge, and therefore enable the conversation to continue as though the presupposition had been known to the hearer all along. Speakers can exploit this to communicate information by the use of presupposition. For instance, (8.26a) presupposes – formally speaking – (8.26b), whereas it actually states (8.26c). However, it's easy to imagine circumstances under which the speaker of (8.26a) intends primarily to communicate the (b) proposition rather than the (c) proposition.

(8.26)   a.   I just found out that Sergey is getting a promotion.
         b.   Sergey is getting a promotion.
         c.   I just found this out.

In typical cases, to presuppose something wouldn't count as "telling" someone something. We couldn't say of the speaker who said "Would you like some more dessert?" that they "told me that I had already had some dessert". However, in (8.26a), we could justifiably say that the speaker "told me that Sergey is getting a promotion". This emphasises the point that the single phenomenon of presupposition covers a lot of ground, from merely establishing the existence of the building blocks required for a sentence to have meaning, all the way to conveying new information in much the same way as a normal assertion would. However, across this range, presuppositions are unified by their behaviour under negation and questioning, which distinguishes them systematically from straightforward entailments.

Summary

Pragmatics is about the use of utterances in context, a particular point of interest being how we manage to convey more than is literally encoded in the semantics of sentences. The additional and different meanings that can be inferred as conversational implicatures save production effort and enable us to "do more with less". Traditionally these have been treated as inferences that we can draw by relying on generalisations about how cooperative speakers tend to behave: however, as we have also seen, another way of looking at these enrichments is to think of them as arising from the hearer's natural tendency to try to find relevance in the utterance they encounter. Another pervasive feature of language is presupposition, which we can think of as the way language expresses assumptions about shared background knowledge: we have seen how presuppositions can be signalled by words and by syntactic constructions, and how the behaviour of presuppositions differs systematically from asserted content. Later in the book we will see how speakers and hearers are able to exploit these enrichments in order to achieve and recognise social goals through the medium of language.

Exercises

1. In the exchange A: "Who's that?" B: "It's me", B's response could appear to be unhelpful. *Me* is a normal way for speakers to refer to themselves, so it appears not to tell A anything that is not obvious. What is it that B probably manages to communicate anyway? Which of Grice's maxims is involved in interpreting the utterance, and why might it be preferable to a more explicit alternative utterance?

2. Consider the utterance "The truth is, continued growth is unsustainable". We are expected to speak truthfully anyway, so why use that claim to lead into a statement? Presumably the speaker is inviting serious attention by explicitly orienting to Grice's quality maxim: 'Perhaps you think I sometimes lie, but I assure you that what I am about to say is true'. Which maxims are similarly evoked by the following statements?[3]

   Continued growth is unsustainable and that's all there is to it.
   Let me make this clear, continued growth is unsustainable.

3. A: "Where are the sociolinguistics books kept?" B: "Psycholinguistics is at the end of the shelf." What might B's utterance implicate, and – with respect to Grice's maxims – how might that arise?

4. Boris Johnson received the "Foot in Mouth" award from the Plain English Campaign in 2004 for the utterance *I could not fail to disagree with you less*. Which of Grice's maxims did Johnson violate? How else could the same proposition have been expressed, and what effect was achieved by the utterance being expressed in the way it actually was?

5. If you hear someone say "It seeped into the basement", you can draw inferences about what kind of substance *it* denotes, and how it entered the basement. What are these inferences? Are they entailments or presuppositions?

6. Under what circumstances would it be possible to say the following things without being committed to the presuppositions (given in brackets)?

Jessica didn't regret arguing with the boss.   (Jessica argued with the boss)

Tom didn't go to Canada again.   (Tom went to Canada before)

Vicky didn't find her keys.   (Vicky lost her keys)

Recommendations for reading

An easy introduction to philosophical accounts of implicature and presupposition is given by Lycan (2000). Kearns (2011) provides a rigorous and detailed, but very readable, treatment of implicature. Relevance Theory, described in detail by Sperber and Wilson (1995), is introduced efficiently by Wilson and Sperber (2002).

Notes

1. For original work by these authors, see Austin (1962), Searle (1979) and Grice (1989).
2. Relevance Theory thus characterises pragmatic enrichments as arising from a cognitive imperative, rather than as a manifestation of rational behaviour in Grice's sense.
3. The idea for this exercise comes from Grundy (2000: 79).

9 Figurative language

Overview

In this book, we have distinguished between semantics, the study of word and sentence meaning in the abstract, and pragmatics, the study of utterances in context. One area of usage in which pragmatics plays a substantial part is in the interpretation of figurative language. Consider (9.1).

(9.1)   My manager is a bulldozer.

If we were to rely wholly on the semantics, we might have to dismiss (9.1) as false – it is not likely to be literally true that the speaker reports to a piece of heavy machinery. But obviously this interpretation doesn't do justice to the speaker of (9.1). What they can naturally be understood to convey is that their manager is, figuratively speaking, a bulldozer: that is to say, the manager is forceful, and perhaps heedless of the feelings of other people.

We might be able to rescue an example such as this by claiming that the literal meaning of *bulldozer* is actually wider than I allowed above, and is perhaps ambiguous between the meaning of "piece of heavy machinery" and "forceful person". However, this approach is not going to extend well to novel uses of metaphor, and in any case we still have to be able to disambiguate between these possible interpretations. So it seems inevitable that pragmatics is going to have to play an important role in the understanding of figurative language.

In this chapter we will look at four kinds of figurative language: irony, metonymy, and (in more detail) metaphor and simile. According to a traditional (and not entirely satisfactory) definition, an ironic utterance is one intended to be taken as conveying the "opposite" of its literal meaning, an idea that links this topic back to the relations of complementarity and antonymy (Section 2.4). Metaphor and simile, however, rely primarily on encyclopedic knowledge rather than knowledge about the meaning relations within language.

Before all this, we need to look a little more closely at the contrast between literal and figurative usage, which is the topic of the following section.

9.1 Literal and figurative usage

We learn word meanings in context, and our representations of word meanings certainly bear connotations picked up from the contexts in which we encountered them. This tends somewhat to blur the distinction between semantic and encyclopedic knowledge. Within the framework known as Cognitive Linguistics, no such distinction is recognised (see Croft and Cruse 2004) – for "Cognitive" linguists, linguistic knowledge is essentially of a piece with other knowledge, as far as its storage and retrieval are concerned. Figurative language, and in particular metaphor, has long been a topic of central importance for Cognitive Linguistics: conceptual metaphors are argued to be a ubiquitous part of human experience. Nevertheless, the approach adopted in this book will follow more traditional semantic and pragmatic lines, largely because there is not space here to do justice to the "Cognitive" enterprise in general, or to explore the arguments raised for and against their position on language in anything like enough detail.

Figurative usage can be inspirationally fresh and original. When figurative uses are recycled to the point of cliché, they frequently settle into the semantic system of the language as new senses for words. Metaphors based on the word *grain* 'seed of cereal' led to an additional sense for *grain*: 'small particle' – of sand, for example. Although historical changes in word meanings are not covered in this book, it is useful to have a scheme that, in principle, could accommodate such processes.

Chapter 1 introduced the idea that people have semantic knowledge simply by virtue of knowing a language – that is to say, they have an understanding of literal meanings. Literal meanings are encoded in the language system and underpin the entailment possibilities of sentences. As discussed in Section 2.2, meaning is compositional: the meanings of sentences derive from the meanings of the component expressions, taking into account the way they have been put together. However, we frequently need to appeal to context in order to understand the meaning that sentences themselves possess, a point made in Section 1.3: for instance, we need to establish what referring expressions refer to, resolve cases of deixis, and so on. The resulting meaning is often called an explicature. If the only word meanings used in the explicature are literal meanings, we can say that the sentence has a **literal interpretation**.

The traditional term **figures of speech** covers various kinds of figurative uses of language, as opposed to literal uses. Grant and Bauer (2004: 51) propose a simple diagnostic test: constructions 'compositionally involving an untruth which can be reinterpreted pragmatically to understand the intended truth' are figurative usage. This appears to capture the intuition that cases such as (9.1) are figurative. However, as Grant and Bauer themselves acknowledge, this test is too restrictive. Stern (2000: 356) cites John Donne's famous words *No man is an island*. Both in its original context and as used idiomatically, this phrase conveys that 'all people are interlinked'. However, this figurative meaning cannot arise because the statement is literally untrue: *No man is an island* is literally true! It is merely so self-evidently true that it would be unlikely to be worth communicating.

We should also be careful in how we interpret the idea that the 'untruth' in a figurative usage 'can be reinterpreted pragmatically'. The traditional point of view about figurative usage has been that it is essentially secondary to literal usage, and arises through pragmatic reinterpretation of literal meanings that are somehow deficient in themselves. Intuitively, we might feel that this is not applicable to certain genres – perhaps, when reading poetry, we have a preference for the figurative interpretation, where one is available. More generally, research on metaphor has suggested that the literal meaning does not necessarily have to be accessed before the figurative meaning (Gibbs 1994; Glucksberg 2008). Under the right circumstances, we can leap straight to the speaker's intended meaning, without being side-tracked by literal meanings when these are obviously irrelevant.

Bearing this in mind, here we will define a **figurative interpretation** as an explicature that involves treating one or more words as if they had meanings different from their literal ones. Context is used not only as a foundation for inferring which referents are being talked about and which senses of ambiguous expressions are likely to be the intended ones, but also to decide whether any words are to be interpreted figuratively. This may be because the literal interpretation yields a sentence meaning that is somehow deviant – untrue, or obvious, or vacuous – or because the context favours a non-literal interpretation. Thus, we do not commit to the idea that the literal interpretation is automatically privileged for the hearer.

Figures of speech should also be distinguished from **idioms**. As Grant and Bauer put it, 'figures of speech can be interpreted according to general cognitive principles, while idioms have to be learnt' (2004: 49). Also outside the category of figurative usage, as defined here, is the innovative creation of new words. This is simply because such words do not have established literal meanings. The first edition of this book used the example of *underwhelmed* as a coinage that was then on its way to being established in English, but which still had the power to surprise the hearer first encountering it: it represents a novel reanalysis of *overwhelmed* as *over-* plus *whelmed*, and the use of this pattern to construct a contrasting word. It was also remarked there that it was probably figurative usage that encouraged the historical meaning change from the Middle English *hwelmen* 'turn upside down' to our *overwhelm* 'overcome'. Now *underwhelmed* has become sufficiently widespread that there has been a further development: the emerging usage of *whelmed* to describe a condition of being neutral or indifferent with respect to something (that is, neither over- nor underwhelmed). This contrasts with the still-extant usage of *whelmed* – drawn more directly from the Middle English source – to mean 'engulfed' or 'submerged'. But while this novel coinage may still have the power to surprise, it still does not qualify as figurative usage for our current purposes.

9.2 Irony

Consider an utterance such as (9.2), appropriate to a rainy day in Edinburgh in June.

(9.2)   Summer is here.

A child who noticed the incongruity of this remark with the weather outside might express surprise at (9.2), and it is conceivable that someone might explain things to the child along the lines of the traditional definition of irony: "They really mean that summer isn't here yet". Such an explanation is of some help: the child has correctly detected the mismatch between the utterance and the situation, and is sensibly advised to treat the explicature of (9.2) as conveying not the literal meaning of the sentence but the negation of it. However, there is more to it than that.

One approach, originally articulated by Sperber and Wilson (1981), sees verbal irony as 'a type of echoic allusion to an attributed utterance or thought' (Wilson 2006: 1724). The idea behind this is that when we utter an instance of verbal irony such as (9.2), we are making as though the thought or utterance was expressed by someone else, or at some other time, and conveying that it is entirely inappropriate for this time. This helps to explain why an utterance such as (9.2) would be appropriate, considered as an ironic statement, if it were made on a rainy day in summer, but inappropriate if it were made on a rainy day in winter, even though the meaning 'summer is not here' would be entirely true of that situation. The essence of this utterance is that it would have been perfectly apt, with no irony intended, if the weather had been fine. An alternative approach, initially developed by Clark and Gerrig (1984), takes verbal irony to be a kind of pretence: the speaker, in a case such as (9.2), is pretending to convey the literal meaning of the utterance, but knows perfectly well that the hearers will see through this pretence.

What these accounts attempt to capture, and what is missing from the traditional approach to irony, is that being ironic does not merely involve saying the opposite of what we mean – rather, it crucially involves some expression of judgement. This point was in fact acknowledged by Grice (1989), who critiqued his own account of irony in terms of violations of the maxim of quality. We do not simply go around making arbitrary false statements under the guise of irony: when we use irony appropriately, it is usually to criticise, mock or object to the statement that we are articulating (and by extension, anyone who said it or would have said it in all sincerity).

9.3 Metaphor, metonymy and simile

Metaphors are traditionally understood as figurative expressions of the form "X is (a) Y" – figurative because they identify their subject with a class of entities to which it does not literally belong. (9.1) was an example of this kind, granting that the speaker's manager is not literally a bulldozer: (9.3) presents some more celebrated examples.

(9.3)   a.   The Lord is my shepherd.   (Psalm 23)
        b.   All the world's a stage.   (Shakespeare, *As You Like It*, II, vii, 139)

        c.   That's . . . one giant leap for mankind.   (Neil Armstrong)

Metaphor has been studied since classical times, and the traditional Aristotelian view regarded metaphors such as these as implicit comparisons ('the world is like a stage'), and so on. In recent linguistic research, this idea has competed with the idea put forward by Glucksberg and Keysar (1990: 3) that metaphors are in fact 'exactly what they appear to be: class-inclusion assertions'.

A question that this debate immediately opens up is whether there are really differences between metaphors and **similes**. Similes are traditionally viewed as figures of speech in which something is said to be *like* something else. Just as in the case of metaphor, it is crucial to the definition that the items being compared are actually substantially different in nature. It is not traditionally regarded as a simile to say *A lemon* *is like a grapefruit,* but it is a simile to say *Running a university department is like herding cats.*

One viewpoint on this question is articulated by Stern, who states that 'similes should be analyzed on the same model as metaphors' (2000: 340). It's certainly the case that there is a striking similarity in meaning between metaphors and their corresponding similes: the examples in (9.4) seem to convey essentially the same meaning as the corresponding metaphors in (9.3).

(9.4) a. The Lord is like my shepherd.
      b. All the world is like a stage.
      c. That is like a giant leap for mankind.

We might think, on this basis, that the difference between metaphor and simile is a superficial one: it is merely that similes contain *like* as an explicit marker of similarity. However, this still leaves us to wonder what the use of *like* is supposed to achieve. The relation that *like* describes is quite a loose one: we can point to two dissimilar things and say that one of them is *like* the other in respect of sharing a particular feature. It seems to be possible to say (9.5), for instance.

(9.5) Humans are like bananas, in that humans and bananas share 50 per cent of their DNA.

We could alternatively try to argue, on the basis of examples like this, that similes are – unlike metaphors – literally true, and in fact not figurative at all, despite appearances.

Setting this question aside and returning to the topic of metaphor, what do we mean if we claim that metaphors are class-inclusion assertions? In essence, we mean that the figurative expression within the metaphor – traditionally called the **vehicle** – is interpreted more broadly than would usually be the case. Thus, in (9.3a), *shepherd* is understood to mean something more like "individual that gives guidance and leadership", in (9.3b) *stage* is understood to mean "location where dramatic events take place" and in (9.3c) *giant leap* is understood to mean "significant instance of progress or development". In (9.1), repeated below, *bulldozer* is understood to mean something along the lines of "powerful and forceful entity that can take actions regardless of the actions of others".

(9.1) My manager is a bulldozer.

To put it another way, on this account, the metaphor vehicles denote superordinate categories that include not only the members of the "literal" category, but also other entities that share certain characteristic properties with the members of the "literal" category. (9.1) then identifies the speaker's manager as literally belonging to this larger category of entities that share some of the characteristic properties of bulldozers. Incidentally, this account posits a clear distinction between metaphors and similes: if we were to say "like a bulldozer" in (9.1), *bulldozer* could still carry its literal meaning and refer only to the usual, smaller category of entities.

Considering the amount of detail that we have had to go into above, in order to specify the meanings of simple metaphorical expressions in literal terms, it is easy to see why metaphors are so effective in communication. Using metaphors, we are able to compress a constellation of attributes into a single expression, perhaps a single word, and then ascribe those properties to the topic of the sentence using a simple copular form (*is, are,* etc.). This economy of expression makes metaphor powerful in poetry, and relevant to scientific theorising as well as to scientific communication.

However, compared with literal language, metaphor places a much greater burden on the hearer, who must be able to identify the relevant points of comparison and discard the irrelevant points. We must be able to work out that, for instance, the speaker of (9.1) is probably trying to convey that their boss is forceful and heedless of others, rather than that their boss pollutes the environment, or is essential to the early stages of projects, or weighs a lot, or costs a great deal, or any of the many other attributes that we might associate with bulldozers and which could at a pinch also be associated with people. For established metaphors, we might have already learnt which set of meanings are likely to be intended by the speaker, but for novel metaphors this is a problem that we have to solve anew – and there are various theoretical accounts of how we do this (see for instance Carston 2010). In the case of poetic metaphors in particular, the intended meaning may be pointed to only very approximately, and the hearer may struggle to identify the features of the metaphor vehicle that are relevant to that intended meaning.

If a metaphorical interpretation is called for, we also have to be able to suppress the literal meaning of the metaphor vehicle. This presents a particular problem in cases where multiple metaphorical expressions are brought together, but their literal meanings are incompatible – a situation traditionally called a "mixed metaphor". Shakespeare's *to take arms against a sea of troubles* is considered an example of this kind: (9.6) presents a couple of even more striking instances.[1]

(9.6)   a.   It is the thin end of a white elephant.
        b.   Mr Dewey would have been wielding a double-edged sword in the shape of a boomerang that would have come back to plague him.

One specific case of metaphor for which the interpretative process is perhaps a little more straightforward is that of **metonymy**: that is, where a person or object is referred to using a metaphorical vehicle whose meaning is closely related. For instance, we can refer to national governments or leaders by the name of the building or location in which they are based or with which they are associated (*The White House/ Downing Street/The Kremlin announced ...*), by the name of the city in which they are located (*Washington announced ...*) or by the name of the country which they govern (*The US announced...*). Another class of metonyms involves identifying groups of people by the garments they wear (*the Green Berets, the Redcaps, the Brownshirts*, and so on).

To be effective expressions, metonym vehicles have to be distinctively related to the people or objects referred to. The vehicle must also be relevant in the context of utterance. For instance, in a bookshop, the authors could be considered to be distinctive features of books, so it would be appropriate to use a category of authors as a metonym for the books they write: *Put more feminist authors in this window*. By contrast, if the context was taking photographs for an interior design magazine, the physical properties of the books would be more relevant: *Fill that shelf with hardbacks*. In either case, it is relatively easy to determine that the objects being talked about are in fact books, rather than authors or parts of books, presumably because the conceptual links between the metonyms and the referents are very strong in these cases.

Summary

This chapter has sketched out some of the major cases of figurative interpretation, and looked briefly at the processes that may underlie those interpretations. Semantically, words and sentences have literal meanings. A literal interpretation of an utterance in context is an explicature that involves only literal meanings, whereas a figurative interpretation is an explicature in which one or more non-literal meanings are involved. However, in some cases, it can be difficult to distinguish between non-literal meanings as opposed to literal meanings that have been extended beyond their original domain, as we saw in the discussion of metaphor versus simile. Figurative interpretation is somewhat open-ended because what is regarded as relevant can vary between different people and between different contexts. For that reason, it offers a powerful and economical means of expression, but is susceptible to misunderstanding, and relies upon the hearer performing additional reasoning in order to recover the speaker's intended meaning.

Exercises

1. Talking of a pair of garden birds in early summer: *They've got two hungry beaks to feed*. What figure of speech is seen in the sentence in italics? What prior knowledge is needed to understand the examples?
2. In Fiji in the 1990s the author had to ask for an explanation of a metaphor *He's a tube light*. Even given that *tube light* means 'fluorescent light', the meaning of this metaphor is quite opaque. Can you guess what it was supposed to convey? What did you need to think about in making a guess, or what kind of information did you lack?
3. Muhammad Ali famously described his own fighting technique with the words *Float like a butterfly, sting like a bee*. Using the technical terms introduced in this chapter, try to identify the figure of speech he was using.
4. In accepting the award for BBC Sports Personality of the Year in 2015, Andy Murray remarked that "A friend sent me an article saying 'Andy Murray is duller than a weekend in Worthing', which I thought was harsh – on Worthing." What kind of figurative language is involved in this remark?

Recommendations for reading

Cruse (2011) is a thoughtful discussion of the topics in the present chapter. Lycan (2000: ch. 14) gives an accessible account of metaphor from the perspective of a philosopher of language. In Huddleston and Pullum (2002: 651ff., 682) there is an informative discussion of dead metaphors among English prepositional meanings. Traugott (2000) provides a short but somewhat technical survey of the roles that metaphor and metonymy play in meaning changes in the history of languages.

Note

1. Denys Parsons, letter in *New Scientist*, 25 March 1971, p. 704.

10 Utterances in context

Overview

Connected utterances make up a **discourse**. By this definition, a discourse might be a conversation, a TV interview, an email, a letter or even a whole book, to the extent that writer and reader keep track of the connections between the utterances in it. This chapter concentrates on one aspect of the pragmatics of discourse, namely how we adapt our utterances to connect them to the current interests and the existing knowledge of the other discourse participants. The language we speak presents us with various ways of packaging information to achieve this purpose – for instance, placing stress on certain material within the utterance, or using one or another distinct syntactic pattern.

The aims of this chapter are limited to making these ideas intelligible and, hopefully, interesting. Discourse pragmatics is a wide field, so the approach taken here is selective.

It is communicatively counterproductive to enter a room in which people are having a conversation and, taking no interest in what they are saying, blurt out whatever you want to tell them. We might make an exception if the information is especially urgent – for example, if there's a fire – but usually this approach is suboptimal. Arguably the major purpose of engaging in communication is to try to update the stock of shared knowledge between speaker and hearer, an idea touched upon at various points earlier in the book. Someone hoping to do this would be well advised to make assumptions about the current state of the discourse and then shape any contribution so as to cohere with this background (rather in the fashion of Grice's Cooperative Principle, as in Section 8.2).

As communicators, we generally have access to a large repository of potential assumptions that we can make about the addressees' knowledge and interests. All humans share an environment (comprising the Earth, Sun and Moon, and so on), and certain traits and dispositions (such as the capacity for pain, for love, and so on). Within a given culture, we share additional norms about how to behave, in a broad sense. We can also generally assume that our interlocutors have opted into the discourse, and so for instance it would be reasonable for me to assume that readers of this book are interested in meaning. We may have past experience of interacting with the addressees, and importantly, as the discourse progresses, we increase our stock of shared experience by adding to it the things that have already transpired in that discourse (what has recently been said by all participants). These all constitute parts of the context of utterance, and when we are interested in pragmatics, we may be interested in how any of these factors influence meaning.

10.1 Definiteness

Definiteness in noun phrases is a significant feature of the grammar of English and will be used as a starting point here. The lists in Table 10.1 give some indication of how definiteness and indefiniteness can be conveyed in English, but don't feel overwhelmed by this list: the discussion here will predominantly focus on *a* and *the*.

The definite article *the* signals that 'this reference is constrained: I am referring to something that you know about'. One class of example is (10.1), which might be spoken by someone phoning from the other side of town.

(10.1)   Look outside, there's a weird green glow in the sky.

According to a common way of thinking about it, the same sky is outside almost everywhere, so the speaker can expect the hearer to know about the sky. That is what makes immediate definite reference appropriate in

Table 10.1 A selection of indefinite and definite forms

Indefinite	Definite
	proper names
	Aberdeen, Zoroaster
determiners	determiners
a, an, some, another, several, most, no, enough, any	*the, this, that, these, those, its, most, their, her, his, your, my, our*
absence when head noun is plural	
_*cities worth visiting,*	
_*famous people*	
indefinite pronouns	personal pronouns
something, someone, somebody, anything, anyone, anybody	*it, they, them, she, her, he, his, you, I, me, we, us*

this case. The sky is a topic, where **topic** is defined as 'what the utterance is primarily about' (Huddleston and Pullum 2002: 236). As we will use the term here, the topic is not the new information presented in the sentence – for example, it is not the weird green glow in (10.1). Instead, topics are entities that are easily accessible given our background knowledge, such as the sky. For a topic there should not be any need to run a preparatory check: "If I were to say *sky*, would you know which one I was talking about?"

A different but common pattern can be seen in (10.2), which is an excerpt from a recipe (intervening material having been omitted here).[1]

(10.2) 675g fresh green beans
        0.5l vegetable oil
        Trim the beans and cut them into . . . 4cm lengths.
        Heat the oil in a wok over a medium-high flame.
        Fry the beans . . . until the skins just begin to crinkle.
        Turn off the heat under the wok.

There is a tendency here for *the* to be used only from second reference onwards. The items introduced as *beans* are subsequently referred to as *the beans*, *them* and *the beans*. *Oil* becomes *the oil*, *a wok* becomes *the wok*, and *a medium-high flame* becomes *the heat*. The first two lines of (10.2) illustrate a feature of recipes: the list of ingredients puts some things into the mind of the reader – makes them into (potential) topics – and after that, definite reference is appropriate whenever the author wants to refer to the same items, which might by then already be gathered on a kitchen worktop.

However, as the *wok* and *flame* examples show, listing items is not the only way to introduce them into the background knowledge applicable to a discourse. These items are mentioned in the discourse, initially through the use of indefinite expressions. At the second mention of *wok*, we naturally understand *the wok* to refer to the same entity as *a wok* did earlier on. In effect, the use of *a wok* introduces the corresponding entity, as a potential topic, into the knowledge base that the hearer is able to consult. The topics are not the words themselves. The expression *the heat* does not contain any of the words present in the expression *a medium-high flame*, but nevertheless constitutes a second reference to the same topic. Upon reading *the heat*, the definite article cues the reader to search through the developing body of background knowledge for this discourse, looking for something already present there which could be referred to by that particular expression. As remarked back in Chapter 3, this includes not only entities that have been specifically mentioned, but also related entities whose existence is inferrable: for instance, once we have introduced *beans* into the discourse, we can refer to *the skins*, using definite reference at first mention, by appeal to the shared background knowledge that beans have skins.

In summary, the examples in (10.1) and (10.2) showed new referents being brought into a discourse by means of indefinite expressions like *a wok* and *675g fresh green beans*. Indefinite marking (here, the determiner *a*, or the absence of a determiner with the plural head noun *beans*) is a signal to the hearer to the effect that 'this entity is new within the mental file that you have opened for this discourse'. An indefinite reference invites the addressee to set up a representation for a referent: in other words, to start treating it as a potential topic.

10.2 Given and new material

We can think of the marking of definiteness or indefiniteness as one device for managing shared background knowledge: specifically, it helps the hearer to understand whether we are talking about established referents or introducing new referents. More generally, English provides us with a variety of strategies that we can use, as speakers, to explain how the meaning that we are communicating relates to already-shared background knowledge. We can think of this as the distinction between **given** and **new** information: that is, between what is already assumed to be known and what the speaker wishes to present for the first time. The following subsections discuss some of these strategies.

10.2.1 Pseudo-clefts

In June 2004 a meteorite fell through the roof of a house in New Zealand and bounced off the sofa. We could describe this truthfully using any of the sentences in (10.3), which are all paraphrases of each other.

(10.3) a. What hit the sofa was the meteorite.
   b. What the meteorite hit was the sofa.
   c. The meteorite hit the sofa.

(10.3c) represents the standard word order for an English declarative sentence. By contrast, the structures in (a) and (b) are called **pseudo-clefts**. Pseudo-clefts have three distinguishing characteristics:

- a clause headed by a "*wh*-word" (we'll call it a *wh*-clause) with an unspecified argument (*what hit the sofa* does not specify the subject, and *what the meteorite hit* does not specify the object)
- a noun phrase that fills in the missing details for the *wh*-clause
- the main verb BE (appearing as *was* in these examples).

Although the *wh*-clauses do not specify their arguments fully, they do presuppose that these arguments exist. For example, both (10.4a) and (10.4b) presuppose (10.4d). By contrast, (10.4c) does not.

(10.4)   a.   What hit the sofa was the meteorite.
         b.   What hit the sofa wasn't the meteorite.
         c.   The meteorite didn't hit the sofa.
         d.   Something hit the sofa.

Consequently, (10.3a) is appropriate in a conversational context in which it is already agreed that something hit the sofa (or potentially in cases where the possibility has been raised that something hit the sofa). It would not be appropriate in contexts in which the idea of anything having hit the sofa is new. For this reason, the exchanges in (10.5a) and (10.5b) seem acceptable, but (10.5c) is odd, unless it has already been established earlier that something hit the sofa.

(10.5)   a.   A: I heard that something hit the sofa.
              B: What hit the sofa was the meteorite.
         b.   A: Did something hit the sofa?
              B: What hit the sofa was the meteorite.
         c.   A: Did the meteorite hit anything?
              B: *What hit the sofa was the meteorite.

In short, then, an appropriate pseudo-cleft is one that matches the conversational background. It does two things: by means of its *wh*-clause it indicates the presupposition, and it presents a noun phrase as the value of the missing argument (that is, it provides specific detail in place of the indefinite *something* in (10.5a) and (10.5b)). The noun phrase carries the new information provided by the utterer of a pseudo-cleft.

10.2.2 It-clefts

(10.6)   a.   It was the childminder who took Judy to the cinema.
         b.   It was Judy who the childminder took to the cinema.
         c.   It was the cinema that the childminder took Judy to.
         d.   The childminder took Judy to the cinema.

It-clefts highlight a noun phrase, often in order to contrast it with another. Although all the examples in (10.6) are paraphrases of one another, they differ in where they place emphasis. For instance, (10.6a) might be used to convey that 'It was the childminder, rather than anyone else, who took Judy to the cinema'.

It-clefts have similar distinguishing traits to pseudo-clefts:

- a clause with an unspecified argument (*who took Judy to the cinema* does not specify the subject, for instance)
- a noun phrase that specifies the missing argument
- the main verb BE (appearing as *was* in these examples)
- *it* as the grammatical subject.

As with pseudo-clefts, the clause with the unspecified variable is presupposed. (10.7a) and (10.7b) both presuppose (10.7d), whereas (10.7c) does not. (The presuppositions are propositions, but to write them down as sentences we need to add an indefinite pronoun, in this example *someone.*)

(10.7)   a.   It was the childminder who took Judy to the cinema.
         b.   It wasn't the childminder who took Judy to the cinema.
         c.   The childminder didn't take Judy to the cinema.
         d.   Someone took Judy to the cinema.

Unlike an entailment, this kind of presupposition is (just about) cancellable: (10.8a) would be flatly self-contradictory, whereas (10.8b) might be usable, particularly in circumstances when someone is demonstrating substantial confusion over the facts.

(10.8)   a.   *The childminder took Judy to the cinema; actually, no one took Judy there.
         b.   It wasn't the childminder who took Judy to the cinema; actually, no one took Judy there.

In situations where reasonably effective communication is taking place, however, speakers would use the *it*-clefts in (10.6) only when the corresponding presuppositions hold true. For example, (10.6a) could be used to reply to the question "Who took Judy to the cinema?", as the asker of this question is clearly also committed to the presupposition that someone took Judy to the cinema.

10.2.3 Passives

(10.9)   a.   The conspirators liked the scheme.
         b.   The scheme was liked by the conspirators.

Sentence (10.9b) is of a type called **passive**. Grammarians call the standard form of the sentence, such as (10.9a), **active**, when contrasting them with passives (see Miller 2002: 26). A passive is generally longer than the corresponding active, because it contains extra grammatical morphemes – BE (showing up as *was* in (10.9b)), the preposition *by* and for some verbs a past participle form. The other obvious difference between actives and passives is that the grammatical subject and object are interchanged between an active sentence and its corresponding passive. However, such pairs of sentences are nevertheless paraphrases of one another, which is true of (10.9a) and (10.9b).

Because the passive construction allows this exchange between subject and object positions, it plays a role in the meshing of new and given information. There is a tendency (although not an invariable rule) in English, and perhaps all languages, for utterances to present given information ahead of new information (Huddleston and Pullum 2002: 1372). Intuitively, this seems like a reasonable way to proceed: start with the knowledge that you already expect the hearer to have, use a topic expression to indicate which bit of that knowledge you want to build on, then present the new information. Thus, in the above example, if the hearer is assumed already to know about the conspirators but not about the scheme, (10.9a) might be preferred, whereas (10.9b) will suit the case in which the hearer is assumed to know about the scheme but not the conspirators.

Another tendency in English usage is one that favours using the subject slot for reference to animate beings, as in (10.9a) (see Biber et al. 1999: 378). On encountering a non-standard form such as (10.9b), the hearer might (if only unconsciously) consider whether this might have been used for a particular communicative reason, as in the discussion of manner implicatures in Section 8.2.4. In this case, the choice of utterance violates the expectation that speakers will use the simplest possible form, and the expectation that the animate referent will be placed in subject position. Why was *the scheme* put in subject position? Perhaps to make it an obvious topic, a crucial link with the background to the discourse. And that might help the addressee to locate a recent memory representation of something that might be describable as a *scheme* but might have been described in different terms in the preceding discourse.

That said, it is worth asking what (10.9) actually presents as new, given that both *the scheme* and *the conspirators* have definite articles and seem to refer to potential topics. In this case, all that is new is that a link is made between the two referents – that the former was *liked* by the latter. In this case, the justification for putting *the scheme* in subject position in (10.9b) might not be that this is the referent already known about by the hearer, but rather that this is the referent of more immediate interest to the hearer at the point of utterance.

Huddleston and Pullum (2002: 1366) discuss and label a variety of additional syntactic structures that can be used to change the way in which English sentences present their information, without actually changing the semantic content (for instance, *The childminder, she took Judy to the cinema*). However, for reasons of space, we will not discuss these various options and their discourse effects any further here.

10.2.4 Lexical and syntactic converses

The previous subsection focused on one of the functions of passives, namely putting arguments into subject position, a basic slot for topics. However, passivisation is not the only way in which this can be accomplished. In Section 2.4 we discussed the sense relation of converseness that holds between some pairs of words. Thanks to this relation holding between the verbs *like* and *please*, (10.10a) and (10.10b) can be regarded as paraphrases of one another.

(10.10)   a.   The conspirators liked the scheme.
           b.   The scheme pleased the conspirators.

This also achieves the function of exchanging the arguments in subject and object position, while preserving semantic equivalence. Just as *like* and *please* exhibit lexical converseness, we can think of active sentences and their corresponding passives as **syntactic converses**. The similarity between syntactic and lexical converseness is further exemplified by (10.11) – the (a) and (b) forms here are paraphrases of one another and of the sentences in (10.10).

(10.11)   a.   The scheme was liked by the conspirators.
           b.   The conspirators were pleased by the scheme.

There are not all that many pairs of converse verbs, however, so this particular alternative to the passive is not generally available for sentences.

10.2.5 Focal stress

As well as lexical and syntactic factors, intonation can also play a role in the way information is packaged. The intonation of spoken English generally gives extra weight to one syllable within a clause (or, more precisely, within an organisational unit that often coincides with a clause). A syllable is a unit of pronunciation, but the kind of stress we are discussing is associated with syntactic units: by default it tends to occur on the rightmost word of a phrase (Giegerich 1992: 252–4), usually a content word.

Focal stress, also known as focus, is syntactically located intonational prominence that does semantic or pragmatic signalling work. Earlier in this book, in the discussion of quantifier scope and of presupposition, there were glimpses of the kind of role that focal stress can play in semantic and pragmatic disambiguation. The present section gives a sketch of its use as a signal of new or contrastive information in pragmatics.

Example (10.12) presents an unremarkable exchange, which shows how focal stress (indicated here by capital letters) marks new information.

(10.12)   A: Did you come by BUS?
          B: I came by TRAIN.

A's use of focal stress indicates that the means of transport ('by bus') is the nub of the query – that is to say, it is the new information being offered for verification. In the context of this conversation, the fact that B arrived at all is likely to be known by both A and B, which makes it acceptable for A to presuppose 'B came by some means'. The focal stress in B's reply conveys that a different kind of transport was used.

The display in (10.13), suggested to me by De Swart and de Hoop (2000: 123), presents a more complicated array of possibilities, to illustrate how focal stress ties in with syntax.

(10.13)   a. Could you   [email [her   [new   BOSS?]]]
          b. No, but I could email   her   new   SECretary.
          c. No, but I could email   her   university.
          d. No, but I could email   MEEna.
          e. No, but I could GO there.

The request in (10.13a) has focal stress on the last word. The different imaginable responses in (10.13b–e) show that what is taken as new could be just the referent of *boss*, as in (10.13b), or any of the different phrases that *boss* is the final word of (*new boss, her new boss* or *email her new boss*). The square brackets in (10.13a) make the point that these phrases are nested inside one another. The response in (10.13d), to take one example, treats the request as presenting *her new boss* as new information, which is signalled by having focal stress on its last word. And, if that is what is new, what is given is the presupposition that the hearer could email someone, which makes "I could email Meena" an appropriate response. It is appropriate because it takes what is presupposed and supplies an argument that fits in as object of the verb *to email*.

Compare (10.12) with (10.14). In (10.14a) the question's focal stress is on *you*. Three different appropriate replies are given as (10.14b–d).

(10.14)   a.   A: Did YOU come by coach?
           b.   B: I came by TRAIN.   (Focal stress on both *I* and
                                              train)
           c.   B: I came by TRAIN.   (Focal stress on *train* alone)
           d.   B: LORna came by coach.

The speaker and hearer are often automatically treated as part of the background (because it is difficult to have a conversation without them), in which case *I* and *you* do not carry focal stress. However, (10.14a) and (10.14b) are examples in which these pronouns can naturally carry stress, to indicate contrast. With the focal stress on *you*, (10.14a) suggests an additional presupposition to the effect that 'you perhaps came by coach and I didn't think you would'. The stressed *I* in (10.14b) conveys something like 'I emphatically deny the possibility that you are apparently thinking of', and the second focally stressed item, *train*, points to train travel as new information that goes against A's supposition that coach travel was a possibility. In this case, atypically, there are two focally stressed items in one clause.

As for the other possibilities, example (10.14c) ignores A's apparent surprise at the possibility of B having come by coach and merely provides information that excludes that possibility. It is a neutral sort of response that lacks the value judgement hinted at by (10.14b). Example (10.14d) does not directly answer A's question in either the affirmative or the negative, but it does give rise to the implicature that B did not come by coach: had B done so, then it would have been appropriate to say so at this point, as discussed in Chapter 8.

10.3 The Question Under Discussion

When we discussed example (10.13), we saw how the same utterance could be interpreted as asking various different questions, depending on what was assumed already to be given and what was taken to be new. One potentially helpful approach to trying to capture precisely what is going on at each move in a conversation, and thus what is being communicated by the discourse participants, is the idea of Question Under Discussion set out by Roberts in 1996 (see Roberts 2012). The **Question Under Discussion (QUD)** is defined as the immediate topic of discussion. This can literally be the question that was asked, but not all information is offered up in conversation just as the response to a question: so we can construe the QUD more broadly as the question that an utterance can be taken to be answering.

On Roberts's account, a QUD "proffers" a set of relevant alternatives, and an appropriate response is one that selects from among this set of alternatives. For instance, a question like "Did Mary come to the party?" proffers alternatives such as "Yes" and "No", whereas a question like "Who came to the party?" proffers lists of names of individuals as its alternatives.

Within the QUD approach, what we understand to be communicated by a given utterance depends on what the QUD is. This is not always obvious, because the question is not always made explicit: sometimes we have to try to infer what the QUD is, based on the properties of the utterance itself (and on information we might have about the discourse context). The reason that the idea of QUD connects to the other concepts discussed in this chapter is that these various techniques for packaging information can be interpreted as signals that the speaker gives to the hearer about what the QUD is.

Consider, for instance, the case of focal stress. As discussed in the previous section, we could consider the focal stress in an utterance like "John came by TRAIN" to be emphasising that *train* is new information, and that in "JOHN came by train" to be emphasising that *John* is new information. However, it's perhaps more straightforward to think of the difference simply in terms of QUD: the former stress pattern suggests that the QUD is "How did John come here?" (or "John came by what?"), whereas the latter suggests that the QUD is "Who came by train?"

By appealing to the QUD, we're able to give an account of how some of the pragmatic enrichments associated with these utterances arise: for instance, "JOHN came by train" may implicate that the speaker did not, because "John and I came by train" would be an appropriate answer to the question "Who came by train?" But "John came by TRAIN" does not implicate that the speaker did not, because that utterance leads us to suppose that the question is "How did John come here?", and that question doesn't invite the speaker to talk about their own travel arrangements.

The idea of QUD is clearly closely related to the notions of given and new information, in that only new information can be the answer to a QUD – in normal conversation we don't tend to ask questions to which we already know the answers. So we can think of "newness", signalled by focal stress – or by any other means – as a possible hint that we can use to figure out what the QUD must have been, in cases where we don't already know this. This in turn could lead us to calculate specific implicatures that depend heavily upon the precise question that was asked.

This is striking in the case of *it*-clefts and pseudo-clefts, for instance (10.6), repeated below.

(10.6)   a.   It was the childminder who took Judy to the cinema.
          b.   It was Judy who the childminder took to the cinema.

    c.   It was the cinema that the childminder took Judy to.
    d.   The childminder took Judy to the cinema.

As remarked in passing earlier, (10.6a) is naturally construed as an answer to the question "Who took Judy to the cinema?" If that is the QUD, we might infer that (10.6a) is an exhaustive answer – that is to say, no one else took Judy to the cinema. This is merely an implicature, and cancellable, but it is nevertheless a distinct meaning that doesn't arise from the other sentences. (10.6b) is naturally construed as an answer to "Who did the childminder take to the cinema?", and as such may implicate that the childminder didn't take anyone else to the cinema, but it doesn't implicate that no one else took Judy there. A similar argument goes for (10.6c). This goes some way towards explaining the intuition about how *it*-clefts and pseudo-clefts are appropriately used in conversation, as outlined in the corresponding subsections earlier.

In a similar spirit, the QUD-based approach might give us a slightly more satisfactory account of examples like (10.9), repeated below.

(10.9)   a.   The conspirators liked the scheme.
           b.   The scheme was liked by the conspirators.

As mentioned earlier, in these sentences, both *the scheme* and *the conspirators* are marked as definite. That being the case, neither the scheme nor the conspirators can be considered "new" here, so we can't readily explain the point of passivising (10.9a) by appeal to the given/new distinction. But we could say that (10.9a) suggests a QUD to the effect of "What did the conspirators think?", while (10.9b) suggests a QUD to the effect of "What did people think of the scheme?" If this is correct, then the sentences might give rise to different implicatures. For instance, suppose that the context for (10.9) is a criminal gang (the *conspirators*) discussing a plan to rob a bank (the *scheme*) and where they will escape to afterwards (the *escape plan*), while (unbeknownst to them) detectives (the *police*) listen in. (10.9a) might then implicate that the conspirators did not like the escape plan, while (10.9b) might implicate that the police did not like the scheme. If this is correct, then the QUD-based approach is potentially useful in explaining the motivation for speakers to produce passive sentences.

In summary, then, the idea of QUD appears to be a potentially useful way of bridging between the grammatical marking of discourse features and the pragmatic consequences of doing so. It is also an intuitively appealing idea. What is not clear at this stage, however, is whether we actually have a mental representation of the notion of QUD – and if so, how we go about constructing it, based on the bits and pieces of information that the discourse provides us with. That is to say, it is not yet clear whether QUD has psychological reality in addition to being a helpful expository device.

Summary

This chapter has presented an introductory survey of some of the structures and devices in English that indicate what the speaker takes to be already known to the hearer when making an utterance, and what the speaker takes to be new. We have discussed definiteness, pseudo-clefts and *it*-clefts, passives and focus marking, but this does not by any means constitute an exhaustive list. We have also considered the notion of Question Under Discussion (QUD), which is one way in which we can try to capture the diverse effects of some of these grammatical manipulations within a unified analysis, and derive predictions about the interpretation of these sentences. However, much more could be said on all of the topics, including the ways in which stress and construction type interact, and the various other approaches that we might take instead of using the given/new distinction as a basis for describing how information is structured in utterances.

Exercises

1. Why is there no need for a preparatory introduction of topic before giving the following warnings: *Keep your head down* and *Mind the step*, where the underlined phrases are definite?
2. Pseudo-clefts can be inverted: for example, *The meteorite was what hit the sofa* as opposed to *What hit the sofa was the meteorite*. Is the presupposition the same or different between these two examples?
3. Tom says that "It was the ATlas that Lucy borrowed". You know that Tom is wrong: (a) Mary borrowed the atlas, and (b) Lucy borrowed the dictionary. Indicate how to correct Tom by filling in the following to make a complete sentence:

   "No, you're wrong: _____".
   Which of the scenarios, (a) or (b), does your completion relate to? How does this fit with the presupposition pattern of *it*-clefts discussed in the chapter?

4. Earlier in the book we discussed how presuppositions can be cancelled: under certain circumstances, a speaker can say *Jessica didn't regret arguing with her boss* without being committed to the

presupposition that 'Jessica argued with her boss'. What kind of Question Under Discussion might license the use of a presuppositional expression like this (... *didn't regret*...), even though the presupposition will later be cancelled?

Recommendations for reading

A comprehensive and readable general account of information packaging is given in chapter 16 of Huddleston and Pullum (2002). De Swart and de Hoop (2000) provide an excellent survey of relevant theories, although parts of this are quite hard, and the same goes for Rooth's (1996) work on focal stress. The idea of Question Under Discussion is set out in full in Roberts (2012).

Note

1. Madhur Jaffrey (1983), *Eastern Vegetarian Cooking*, London: Jonathan Cape, p. 18.

11 Doing things with words

Overview

What is the point of communicating? That may seem like a strange question to ask at this stage of a book. But most of the chapters so far have focused primarily on utterances that make statements of fact. Stating – passing on facts that will be news to our addressees – is certainly an important function of language, but it is not the only one. Much of what we do in language is not reducible to the act of stating: we exchange greetings, we ask questions, we issue requests, we apologise, we complain, we warn, we thank, and much else besides.

J. L. Austin was one of the first researchers to focus attention on this question. His 1955 lecture series, published posthumously in 1962 under the title *How to Do Things with Words*, made the point that – in contrast to the assumptions of the then-prevailing positivist view – relatively few of the things uttered in natural language could actually be said to be "true" or "false". This, however, is not to say that the utterances are not meaningful, rather that we need to analyse them in a different way, specifically in such a way as to reflect their force as social actions.

In this chapter, we will consider briefly what kinds of social action can be performed through the medium of language, and how speakers and hearers manage to perform and recognise these actions.

11.1 Speech acts

Here we will follow Searle (1975, 1979) in using the term **speech acts** to describe the basic units of linguistic interaction: that is to say, the things that we can accomplish through the use of language. (11.1) lists a small sample of speech acts, along with examples of sentences that could be uttered in order to bring them about.

(11.1) a. statement: "I lived in Edinburgh for five years."
        b. order: "Pay this bill immediately."
        c. question: "Where are you from?"
        d. prohibition: "No right turn."
        e. greeting: "Hello."
        f. invitation: "Help yourself."
        g. felicitation: "Happy New Year!"
        h. apology: "I'm terribly sorry."

It has proved difficult to develop an exhaustive list of possible speech acts: Austin (1962) reckoned that there could be several hundred distinct entries on such a list. Austin zoomed in particularly on a category of items that he called **performative**, which appear to have the property to perform social acts merely by virtue of being uttered, under the appropriate contextual conditions. The examples in (11.2) are of this type.

(11.2) a. I name this ship the *Queen Elizabeth*.
        b. I now pronounce you husband and wife.
        c. I apologise for my lateness.

The speaker of (11.2a) performs the action of naming the ship by saying these words. Of course, in practice, saying these words will only have the effect if the speaker is authorised to perform the action. The same is true of (11.2b). In the case of (11.2c), unlike the other examples, the action will be successfully performed by any (sincere) utterance of the words, as there are no social conventions governing who may and may not apologise for their own lateness.

A proposed diagnostic for performative utterances is that the word *hereby* can be inserted before the verb. It would be coherent to say "I hereby apologise" but not, for instance, to say "I hereby sing". By this definition, there are many performative or potentially performative verbs in English, including *apologise, complain, protest, resign, object, declare, open, close, vote, propose*, and so on. It is not entirely clear whether these automatically constitute distinct acts, or whether they could naturally be grouped into distinct classes. Various researchers have attempted to do this on more or less principled grounds; in recent years, work in computational linguistics has paid attention to this issue, as it is relevant for building and training artificial dialogue systems.

It is also not clear whether the kinds of speech act that we might naturally group together are best understood as the same sort of thing. Take the case of questions. In the following section, we will see that distinguishing questions from other kinds of speech act is not entirely straightforward, but let's suppose that we can do this. Then we can consider (11.3) as showing various different examples of questions.

(11.3)   a.   What's your name?
         b.   Is today Tuesday?
         c.   Today's Tuesday, isn't it?

We can think of all these as information-seeking questions: the speaker is performing the social action of trying to obtain information from the hearer. Yet there are systematic differences between the three examples. (a) is a *wh*-question, and admits arbitrarily many possible answers. (b) is essentially a yes/no question, also called a "polar" question, and admits only the answer "yes" or "no" (although the hearer could opt out of answering by saying "I don't know"). (c) is also a yes/no question but seems to encode the fact that it has a preferred response, namely "yes". This kind of question is sometimes called a "check-question". Although we could characterise what the speaker of any of these sentences was doing as "asking a question", it's not obvious that these three utterances are really performing the same social action. For instance, if we were to categorise them by the kind of response that they elicit from a cooperative hearer, we might come to the conclusion that they were different things. And looking at the effect on the hearer would seem to be a reasonable way of trying to determine what kind of social action is being performed.

   We can characterise speech acts at several different levels of organisation. Austin proposed a distinction between locutionary, illocutionary and perlocutionary acts. In this scheme, approximately speaking, locution covers what was actually said, illocution what was meant and perlocution the effect that the utterance had. Suppose we are at dinner and you ask me to pass the salt by saying the words "Could you pass the salt?", and as a result of this I do so. We could report this in several different ways. As a locutionary act, we would describe it as follows: "You said 'Could you pass the salt?'" As an illocutionary act, we would describe it as: "You asked me to pass the salt". As a perlocutionary act, we would describe it as: "You got me to pass the salt". Here we are focusing on the illocutionary level, but it is sometimes useful to know what is and is not considered to fall within the jurisdiction of speech act theory.

11.2 Sentence types and other indications

For speech acts to be effective, hearers have to be able to recognise them as such. Other conditions also have to hold – for instance, hearers have to be willing to comply with them – but a failure to recognise a speech act as, say, a request will probably prevent it from achieving its intended outcome. The problem of speech act recognition turns out to be a difficult one, despite the availability of various indications or cues of speech act type, as we shall see.

11.2.1 Syntactic cues and indirect speech acts

One major category of cues to speech act type is syntactic. The speech acts in (11.1a–c) were placed at the head of the list because they correspond with the three major sentence types of English (and many other languages). These sentence types are **declarative**, commonly associated with statements; **interrogative**, commonly associated with questions; and **imperative**, commonly associated with orders. In English these sentence types are clearly distinguished syntactically, as the example sentences for (11.1a–c) illustrate.

Nevertheless, there are two limitations to attempting to identify speech act types on the basis of syntactic cues. As discussed above, there are potentially many more distinct speech act types than just these three, and it is clear that these other types cannot always be distinguished just by syntactic considerations. The sentences *I promise you that . . .*, *I warn you that . . .* and *I advise you that . . .* all use the same syntactic frame and are distinguished just by the lexical items involved. But even if we just restrict ourselves to statements, questions and orders (and we assume that questions represent a single speech act type), it turns out that the mapping from sentence type to speech act type is somewhat inconsistent. (11.4) illustrates this.

(11.4)   a.   I'd be grateful if you would close the window.
         b.   Could you close the window?
         c.   Close the window.

Formally, (11.4a) is a declarative sentence: it expresses an aspect of the speaker's state of mind; (11.4b) is an interrogative; and (11.4c) is an imperative. Yet all three appear to be used to perform the same speech act, in this case a request. When a sentence type is used to perform a speech act that is not customarily associated with it, we have what is called an **indirect speech act** (see Searle 1975). By this definition, (11.4a) and (11.4b) are examples of indirect speech acts. They are by no means unusual: Levinson (1983) argues that the majority of speech acts are in fact indirect. Certainly, we might think that (11.4c) represents an unusually brusque way of trying to bring about the effect of getting the hearer to close the window, and would only be appropriate if the action was a matter of urgency.

There are several accounts of how we could get from the "literal" speech act associated with a sentence to the indirect speech act that it performs. Consider the interpretation of (11.4b) as a request, rather than as a question enquiring into the hearer's capability to close the window. Gordon and Lakoff (1971) propose that, in such a case, the speaker already knows that the answer to the question is "yes", and the hearer knows this: consequently, the hearer can infer that the purpose of the utterance is not simply to ask a question, and has to arrive at a different interpretation. Searle (1975) offers a slightly more detailed account: he argues that asking the question (11.4b) signals that the answer (known to be "yes") is relevant to the speaker. The hearer can infer that the reason it is relevant whether the hearer can close the window is that the speaker wants the hearer to do so. For that reason, the question can be reinterpreted as an indirect request.

We can construct some kind of rationale for various other cases of indirect speech act interpretation, initially acting as though the literal interpretation is intended, and subsequently performing additional reasoning when the literal interpretation leads us into apparent absurdity. However, since the 1970s, the consensus opinion seems to have moved away from the idea that we actually do this – perhaps the syntactic cues are not quite as privileged as this kind of account would suggest.

11.2.2 Lexical cues

In the case of performative verbs, it is clear that the presence of particular lexical items signals the presence of particular speech acts (leaving aside the question of whether every different performative verb signals a different speech act, as touched upon earlier). These are not entirely reliable signals: we can use performative verbs in non-performative ways. For instance, we can use them to report the performative actions of others: if I say *She named the ship*, that is clearly a statement rather than an act of naming in itself. Nevertheless, when we encounter a performative verb in the present tense and in a sentence in which the subject is the speaker, we can be reasonably confident about the speech act being performed.

In other cases, we might find particular non-performative lexical items to be useful indicators of the kind of speech act that is being performed. Consider the *Could you . . .* of (11.4b). In terms of its semantic meaning, this appears to suggest that the sentence is going to ask about the hearer's capability to do something (perhaps politely or hypothetically, given the use of *could* instead of *can*). However, experience suggests that *Could you . . .* is an idiomatic way of making a polite request, just as *Why not*... is an idiomatic way of making a suggestion. This could be because the reasoning outlined in the previous subsection has been somehow routinised by hearers, or it could be that through encountering many instances of *Could you*... being used in requests we have simply learned that that is a potential use for these words. In either case, a competent user of English is entitled to think it somewhat likely that an utterance beginning *Could you*... will constitute an indirect request.

There are, of course, even more obvious lexical markers of particular kinds of speech act that are also not performative verbs. *Sorry* as a marker of apology is perhaps the most obvious; *hello* is maybe even more emphatic as a marker of greeting, and its other uses in dialogue are rather marginal. Although there are ways of greeting without saying *hello*, the use of this particular lexical item is reasonably reliable as an indicator that what is taking place is an act of greeting. In the middle of an established interaction, saying "hello" is blatantly anomalous.

We might even be able to use smaller pieces of semantic information than that to help us identify the speech act being performed. Some speech acts, for example, relate predominantly to the speaker: if I *protest*, or *resign*, for instance, I do so largely without the involvement of the hearer. Even an *apology* doesn't have to be clearly directed towards a particular recipient. However, for other speech acts, such as *requesting* or *advising*, it is clear that the purpose of the act is to effect some kind of change on the mental state of a particular hearer. We might conjecture, therefore, that speech acts involving first-person pronouns (*I*, *we*) are likely to be of one of the former types, while those involving second-person pronouns (*you*) are a little more likely to be of one of the latter types.

11.2.3 Discourse cues

One of the reasons that the utterance "Hello" is likely to be perceived as anomalous in the middle of a conversation is that it is customarily used to perform the speech act of greeting, but that speech act is only really appropriate at the beginning of a conversation. More broadly, we have access to a potentially rich set of knowledge about how interactions take shape, including the kinds of social actions that are likely to be performed during them, and the interdependencies that can exist between those social actions.

One example that we've already discussed in this book is the fact that there tends to be a close dependency between questions and answers. There is clearly a logical dependency here – something cannot be an answer unless it corresponds to a question – but there is also a rich expectation that questions are almost immediately followed by answers. As discussed in Chapter 8, we will naturally try to interpret something as an answer if it is said in response to a question – (11.5) presents another example of this. Moreover, if there is no answer forthcoming, we will readily interpret silence as communicatively meaningful: even a short silence in response to A's utterance in (11.5) could be interpreted as indicating a wish on B's part to decline the invitation.

(11.5) A: Would you like to go for a coffee with me?
        B: I have to finish this assignment.

In this case, in speech act terms, A's utterance can be understood as an invitation, and the specific expectation here is that B's response will either be to accept or decline the invitation. Similarly, if A's utterance constitutes an offer, we will expect B either to accept or decline the offer. And, just as in the general question–answer case, we can use this expectation to help us understand B's utterance: even if it doesn't superficially appear to serve the purpose of responding to A's utterance, we will try to enrich it pragmatically by appeal to our background assumptions in order to make it interpretable as an appropriate response.

This idea was developed by Schegloff and Sacks (1973). They used the term **adjacency pair** to describe the relationship between two conversational turns that are highly likely to happen sequentially, such as question–answer. When we encounter the first part of an adjacency pair being performed as a speech act, we can quite strongly expect that the next speech act will be the second part of the adjacency pair. Clark (2004) argues that this kind of relation can also exist between wordless communicative acts such as gestures, raising the issue of whether we can have things like question–answer sequences playing out in purely gestural communication. However, we won't delve further into that possibility here (see Clark 2012 for more discussion).

We can also use higher-level information about the status of the discourse to tell us something about the kind of speech act that is being performed. The fact that greetings go at the beginning of conversations is potentially helpful in recognising something as a greeting. Unlike many languages, English doesn't have an all-purpose expression that serves both to open and close conversations – although *ciao* has been borrowed in from Italian and seems to fulfil this dual function in English too. Importantly, assuming that the opening and the closing of a conversation are essentially different social acts, it is nevertheless easy to tell which one is being performed by a particular utterance of "ciao" – if there isn't currently a conversation going on between speaker and hearer, it's a greeting, and if there is, it's rather likely to be a conversation ender or "leave-taking" device.

But there are many other pieces of knowledge available to us about the possible actions at a given stage in a conversation, and it seems likely that we use this to constrain our guesses as to the speech act being performed by a speaker. For instance, if someone says their own name, they could be introducing themselves, but this is only a possible interpretation if there are people present who do not know them (or who might not know them). If a customer goes into a restaurant and says "table for two", that's analysable as a request, but if the waiter says it to the customer first, it's analysable as something more like a check-question. There is not space here to scratch the surface of all the knowledge we have that is potentially relevant to the identification of speech acts, but it might be helpful to be able to identify some broad classes of relevant knowledge, as that offers us some basis for thinking about the processes that are going on under the surface. That will be the topic of the following, final subsection of this book.

11.2.4 Integrating the information

How do we take these various sources of information about speech acts – along with other potential sources of information not discussed above, such as prosody, gesture, and so on – and use them to determine which speech act is being performed? As we discussed earlier, a traditional approach holds that we initially read the speech act directly off the syntax, and then perform pragmatic enrichments to correct this if it gives us some kind of anomalous outcome. But, as we've also seen, this idea is problematic: it only accounts for a relatively small portion of the possible speech acts in the system (those associated with distinct sentence types). Also, on psycholinguistic grounds, this is a somewhat implausible approach, as it suggests that we have to perform a lot of pragmatic reasoning in order to understand the purpose of utterances, and yet in practice we are able to recognise indirect speech acts very rapidly. If someone says "Could you pass the salt?", a cooperative interlocutor passes the salt, rather than whiling away seconds thinking about how to explain this apparent question as some other kind of utterance.

There are at least a couple of other broad approaches to this problem. The plan-based approach, initially laid out by Perrault and Allen (1980) and elaborated in much subsequent work, argues that what hearers are doing is trying to recognise the goals of the speaker and to cooperate in their achievement. From this perspective, the speaker is seen as a rational agent trying to bring about certain changes in the world that they find desirable – which sounds rather grandiose, but in practice could be something as simple as causing a currently open window to be closed. The speaker then constructs a plan to achieve these changes, which may involve performing speech acts. The hearer is able to draw inferences about what the speaker seems to be doing at a given point in time, and use these to derive conclusions about what the speaker wants to be the case; but also the hearer can use their understanding of the speaker's likely goals to draw conclusions about what the speaker is trying to do. This approach is appealingly general, as an account of interaction, but when applied in detail to even relatively simple examples it seems to involve a lot of work.

The dominant approach in the computational literature over the past thirty years or so has been the alternative "cue-based" approach. The idea here is that we simply consider all the evidence that could bear upon the question of what speech act is being performed (syntax, words, context, etc.), weigh this evidence probabilistically, and thus arrive at a guess as to the speech act that is most likely to be taking place. In practice, it seems rather unlikely that we actually use all this information, and it's not clear how we represent some of it (how do we keep track of what is likely in a given conversation, for instance?). However, this approach has proven fruitful for small-scale artificial dialogue systems.

Ultimately, the question of which kind of approach is better is a psychological (or in some cases a practical) one, and discussing this problem in more detail takes us some way beyond the scope of this book. But as far as the description of speech acts in English is concerned, this is still an informative debate. We seem to have good evidence that speech acts are signalled by a range of linguistic devices, doubtless including syntax, but with syntax not playing such a central role as suspected by Searle and colleagues in the 1970s. It also seems that the recognition of speech acts depends on context, but here we are not talking just about the linguistic context but also the cultural context; and it seems that encyclopedic knowledge about how the world works plays an important part in this kind of discourse pragmatics. If we take the treatment of speech acts to be a part of linguistic semantics and pragmatics, it becomes increasingly difficult to draw a clear boundary between linguistic knowledge and world knowledge.

Summary

The idea that we can achieve social actions through the use of words is perhaps the essential reason why linguistic communication is so crucial for our species. Many distinct actions can be performed in this way. In one broad category of sentences, called performatives, the verb explicitly identifies the social action that the speaker is performing (such as *promise* in sentences beginning "I hereby promise . . ."). However, in most cases, the intended purpose, or illocutionary force, of the sentence is not explicitly marked and must be inferred. Syntactic features of the sentence, such as the sentence type, are a helpful cue to this, but many speech acts are indirect, in the sense that their purpose does not correspond to the "typical" purpose for the sentence type. Although theories differ as to how we take into account all the information that might be of use to us, it seems clear that in practice we draw upon many distinct linguistic and non-linguistic factors when we perform the task of recognising the purpose of an utterance (a task we perform almost every time we use language).

Exercises

1. Using the notions of speech acts and presupposition, give a brief description of the wording of this notice seen in a bus: "Thank you for not smoking. MAXIMUM FINE £100." (In the same frame there was a picture of a cigarette with a slash through it, inside a red circle that indicates mandatory prohibition.)
2. For each of the following, name the kind of direct speech act that would "normally" be associated with the sentence, given its sentence type, and say what indirect speech act the example would probably be used to perform.

   (a) Can't you stop talking?
   (b) Help yourself to milk and sugar.
   (c) Have you heard, our team's leading 18 to 15?
   (d) You have my sympathy.
   (e) Don't imagine that entailment and implicature are the same thing.
   (f) Accept my profound condolences.
   (g) Have I ever let you down?
   (h) I recommend that you keep a copy of the letter.

3. What kind of function does the politeness formula "I should let you go" tend to serve in a conversation? How can we explain this effect?

Recommendations for reading

Lycan (2000) and Saeed (2015) offer good introductory treatments of speech acts. Searle (1975) is worth reading as a more detailed treatment of how indirect speech acts can be calculated from a literal starting point. Chapter 5 of Levinson (1983) is also a good guide to the problem of speech act identification, and the limitations of Searle's approach. Jurafsky (2004) gives a lucid account of the competing approaches to the recognition of speech acts from a computational perspective.

Suggested answers to the exercises

Chapter 1

1. *Arriving* denotes a change from not *being in/at* a place to *being in/at* it. *Leaving* denotes the reverse transition: from *being in/at* a place to not *being in/at* it. In parallel to this, *learning* can denote a transition from a state of not *knowing* to *knowing* something, and *forgetting* is the reverse transition from *knowing* to not *knowing*. Establishing this parallel involves considering word meanings without regard to context, and is therefore part of semantics.

2. Although we cannot be certain, it's reasonable to infer that the grade was probably low. By not making a more strongly positive statement such as "You did very well", the tutor can naturally be seen to suggest that the student's grade was near the threshold for failure – that is to say, the most positive thing that could be said about it was that it wasn't a fail. However, the tutor's utterance is still compatible with the student having done well: we could, for instance, imagine a situation in which the tutor is only allowed to tell students whether or not they failed, until the official results are released. Or it could be that the tutor thinks that the student is especially worried about the possibility of failure, and wants above all to dispel that worry. Because we are considering alternative utterances that could have been used, this is pragmatic reasoning (which usually gives rise to uncertain conclusions).

3. *Pick the right lock* can mean 'choose the correct lock' or 'without a key, open the correct lock'. At least two different propositions are involved, one for each possible meaning that the sentence can have. We could arrive at still more distinct meanings – and more distinct propositions – by also considering the ambiguity of the words *right* ('correct' vs 'located to the right-hand side') and *lock* ('security device', 'installation on a canal', 'piece of hair', etc.). *Pick the right lock* might also mean 'choose the canal lock on the right-hand side'.

4. The *kangaroo* case is a classic example of the limits of ostension: if we do not understand the language that someone else is speaking, then pointing towards something while a word is said does not constitute reliable evidence that the word has anything to do with the name for that thing. They could be expressing an entirely unrelated sentiment, such as 'I don't understand you', or talking about a property of the thing such as its size or colour, or indeed naming a part of it. To resolve this, we would either need to know how the word *kangaroo* is used in a broader range of contexts (is it always associated with this class of animals?) – or, better still, we would need to understand the language that was being spoken, because then we could ask about the meaning of the word.

5. The sign clearly isn't supposed to mean that carrying a dog is a precondition for using the escalator. Nor does it impose an obligation on people to take care of dogs for which they wouldn't usually be responsible, while on the escalator. Essentially, the sign means to convey that people who have dogs with them when using the escalator should carry those dogs. The deictic *your* could be added to this, with an optional *by you*, to indicate precisely which dogs (relative to the hearer) need to be carried, and optionally who is responsible for doing that: *Your dogs must be carried (by you) on this escalator.* In practice, this seems like overkill because no competent user of language would really misunderstand the intention behind the original sign.

Chapter 2

1. *Distrust, disregard* and *dislike* can be glossed respectively as 'not trust', 'not regard' and 'not like'. In these cases, the verb itself falls within the scope of *not*. *Disprove* and *dissuade* can be glossed as 'prove not (to be the case)' and 'persuade not (to do)'. In these cases, the verb does not fall within the scope of *not*, although other material in the sentence meaning does.

2. The incorrect analysis of *not good enough* corresponds to the bracketing '(not good) enough'. In fact, the usual bracketing for this expression would be 'not (good enough)'. *Good enough* means 'adequate' and here it falls into the scope of *not* and is negated, so *not good enough* means 'inadequate'. (The negation encoded by *not* can alternatively be encoded by the negative prefix *in-*, which fits with *adequate*.)

3. The intended meaning of the sentence could be represented as 'we (don't like (the same things))', as opposed to 'we (don't (like the same things))'. On the latter interpretation, the meaning of the sentence would be that it is not the case that the speaker and hearer like the

same things. This interpretation would be odd given the preceding context, the speaker having just said that 'You and I are well suited', unless one or other of the sentences was intended ironically. However, there are alternative utterances that would have removed the ambiguity entirely: for instance, the speaker could have said *We dislike the same things*. This only admits the first of the two interpretations discussed above: when the concept of 'not liking' is expressed by the single word *dislike*, its status as a constituent is not in doubt.

4. (b) entails (a): we could argue that there is a sense of *love* that doesn't entail *like*, but that is not the sense of *love* that is usually applicable to the relation between students and a course, even at the best of times. (c) and (d) entail each other: they are paraphrases.

5. (a) They were soundless. (b) They were silent. (c) They were noiseless. (a) $\Rightarrow$ (b), (a) $\Rightarrow$ (c), (b) $\Rightarrow$ (a), (b) $\Rightarrow$ (c), (c) $\Rightarrow$ (a), (c) $\Rightarrow$ (b).

6. *Awake* and *asleep* can be considered complementaries because *She is awake* entails that *She is not asleep* and *She is not asleep* entails that *She is awake*. (Furthermore, *She is not awake* entails that *She is asleep* and *She is asleep* entails that *She is not awake*: these are logical consequences of the first two entailments.) I take *half-awake, half-asleep* and *dozy* to denote different ways of being awake, rather than denoting an intermediate region between 'awake' and 'asleep'. Note, for instance, that *He's dozy but still awake* is not semantically problematic, but *He's dozy but still asleep* is awkward; and that, in response to someone saying "You're asleep", it's acceptable to respond "No, but I admit I'm dozy/half-asleep/only half-awake".

7. Of this set of words, the immediate hyponyms of *footwear* seem to be *shoes, slippers* and *boots*. *Sneakers* and *trainers* are synonyms, and these along with *sandals* are hyponyms of *shoes, galoshes* is a hyponym of *boots*. Although *shoes* enters into this hierarchy at a level at which it contrasts with *boots* and *slippers*, there is potentially another sense of *shoes* in which it could be considered roughly synonymous with *footwear*, and used in its place as a superordinate: for instance, we would normally go to a *shoe shop* rather than a ?*footwear shop* to buy boots and slippers as well as shoes in the narrower sense of the word.

Chapter 3

1. We could think of a prototypical *shoe* as having an *upper*, a *sole* and a *heel*, although we could also think of the *heel* as being a part of the prototypical *sole*. The prototypical *upper* has a *tongue*, and possibly some kind of fastener, although there is not an obvious superordinate term for the various incompatible possibilities (*laces, buckle, Velcro*, etc.).

2. Under this set of definitions, *side* is a superordinate for *top, bottom, front* and *back*. The description names these as four different kinds of *side*, and the relation of incompatibility holds between them because they are introduced with different and incompatible descriptions. However, if we wanted also to use the word *side* in the familiar way, to describe the spatial part that is neither the *top*, the *bottom*, the *front* or the *back*, we would have to consider this to be a distinct sense of *side* that is a hyponym of the more general sense of *side* used here.

3. Count senses of these words are illustrated by *There is a paper on my desk, How many glasses shall I wash?* and *Whole cheeses are on sale at that stall*. Mass senses are illustrated by *We use too much paper, It can be expensive to recycle glass* and *Cheese is made from milk*. In the count sense, taking *paper* to mean 'newspaper' (rather than, say, conference paper), its hyponyms include *broadsheet* and *tabloid* (and more recently *Berliner*, as well as *freesheet*, and so on). Hyponyms of *glass* in the count sense include *goblet, wineglass, tumbler*, and so on. Hyponyms of *cheese* include any kind of cheese that is formed in distinct units: a *Brie*, a *cheddar*, an *Edam*, and so on. In the mass sense, hyponyms of *paper* include *newsprint, printer paper*, and so on. Hyponyms of *glass* include *window glass, bulletproof glass* and *safety glass*. Hyponyms of *cheese* include *Brie, cheddar* and *Edam*, but also types of cheese that do not form distinct units, such as *cottage cheese, soft cheese*, and so on. As a generalisation, the mass nouns (including the hyponyms) denote materials or substances. The count nouns (including the hyponyms) denote kinds of thing: newspapers, drinking vessels and formats in which cheese is produced.

4. In *Have you ever eaten rabbit?*, the noun *rabbit*, which would normally be a count noun, is "coerced" into a mass noun interpretation in which it denotes a substance. If the article *a* were present, this reading would be difficult to obtain. Although the idea of rabbit as a foodstuff is not all that exotic, the same coercive reading seems to be available if we replace *rabbit* by, say, *bear* or *crocodile*.

5. As discussed in the chapter, *to the left of* is generally ambiguous, in that it's not clear whether the speaker means 'to the left from the speaker's perspective', 'to the left from the hearer's perspective' or 'to the left from the perspective of the object being used as a reference point'. However, unlike chairs, stools do not tend to have an intrinsic orientation – they are more symmetrical than chairs, and lack a back – so what would be meant by 'to the left from the perspective of the stool' is impossible to determine. (I assume that 'to the left from the perspective of the chair' effectively means 'to your left, if

you were sitting on the chair the normal way round'.) Consequently, *to the left of the stool* can't really be used that way, and realistically has to mean 'to the left from the speaker's perspective' or 'to the left from the hearer's perspective'. In that sense, it's actually slightly less ambiguous than *to the left of the chair*.

Chapter 4

1. The adjectives for which *quite* is a downtoner are gradable: it makes sense to talk in terms of the extent to which someone or something is *clever, late, small* or *unusual*. These could, for instance, also be modified by *very*, which would convey a stronger meaning than *quite* in each case. The adjectives for which *quite* is a maximiser are not gradable: you could think of them as corresponding to the endpoints of scales. They can't be modified by *very* but they could be modified by *completely*. It's just about possible to imagine *quite* acting as a maximiser on a word like *clever*, but there seems to be a strong preference for interpreting it as a downtoner (at least in British English) when the opportunity presents itself (that is, when the adjective is gradable).

2. The adjectives *young, rude, unpalatable, tasty* and *weak* seem generally to yield biased *how*-questions. *Old, polite* and *strong* do not, in general. *Tasty* seems to give rise to a biased question where *palatable* would not, perhaps because it is a stronger positive adjective than the "neutral" alternative.

3. Taking *royal visitor* to mean 'a royal person who is visiting', this admits a straightforward intersective analysis. *Royal correspondent* would normally mean 'journalist who reports on royalty', and on that reading is not intersective, because the meaning contributed by *royal* can only be understood relative to the domain of *correspondent*. If, on the other hand, we meant the phrase to mean 'a royal who writes letters' (*Queen Christina was Descartes' royal correspondent*), an intersective analysis would work. *Heavy eater* is not intersective, as it means 'someone who eats heavily' rather than 'someone who eats and is heavy'. We can be reasonably confident about this because *eater* is hardly ever used as a free-standing expression to mean 'someone who eats'. *Wise fool*, in order to be understood as a non-contradictory expression, must mean 'a professional fool (i.e. clown or jester) who is wise', and can therefore be interpreted intersectively.

4. When we describe Proxima Centauri as *small, cool, red* and *near*, we intend these adjectives to be interpreted relatively, and specifically with reference to the standards by which we judge stars. However, when we describe it as the *closest* other star to the Sun, this is an

absolute description, and holds irrespective of whether or not we consider the actual distance involved (4.24 light years) to be large or small.

Chapter 5

1. Compared with *The minister made the civil servant resign*, the sentence ? *The minister resigned the civil servant* is a single clause, and we would expect it to encode direct causation (whereas the two-clause causative *made . . . resign* can encode either direct or indirect causation). Given the lengthy gap between the minister's announcement and the civil servant's actual resignation, it seems more likely that the causation was indirect – that is, that the minister's announcement did not by itself have the effect of causing the civil servant to resign. That being the case, *resigned* isn't intended as a causative verb in the question ? *Who is going to be resigned next?* The question cannot be analysed as meaning 'Who will be made to resign next?', but something more like 'Whose resignation will be announced, without it actually having taken place, next?' The apparent ill-formedness of the question is an effective way of getting people to think about the meaning of the word *resign*, and potentially to reflect upon the minister's apparent high-handedness.

2. Humpty was 'together' (intact) before his 'great fall'. The soldiery failed in the task of getting Humpty back into this previous state of togetherness. *Put* is a causative verb, and the restitutive adverb *again* modifies an embedded proposition 'Humpty is together', rather than the main clause action verb *put*.

3. Sentences (a) and (b) are unaccusative, because the referent of the subject does not consciously carry out the action, as confirmed by the peculiarity of these sentences with *carefully*: * *The kite carefully flew*, * *My heart carefully sank*. Sentence (c) is unergative: reading is something that students do consciously and they can do it carefully.

4. As discussed in the chapter, *give* requires three arguments, corresponding to a giver (Agent), a Recipient and something to be given (Theme). We can think of *pay* as representing a specific case of giving something, usually money, in return for goods or services rendered. Perhaps because the verb *pay* encodes information about the Theme, this does not need to be made explicit in the sentence, although it can optionally be specified. Thus we can say *John paid Mary* or *John paid Mary £1,000*, whereas we cannot say * *John gave Mary* although we can say *John gave Mary £1,000*. In fact, as the contrast between *John paid Mary* and *John paid the bill* indicates, we can even omit the Recipient

with the verb *pay*. *Mary* fulfils the role of Recipient, but *the bill* is more like a Theme (we can't say **John paid the bill £1,000*). If the Theme and Recipient are both inferrable, we can use *pay* in what looks like an intransitive construction (*We went to the restaurant; John paid*), although there is some debate about whether these various senses of *pay* are really analysable as the same verb.

Chapter 6

1. *Recently* goes with the past time group that includes *yesterday*. Note the unacceptability of **He is happy recently*, **He shops at the corner store recently*, **I will do it recently*. (We noted that *recently* can be used with present perfect forms such as *I have been there recently*, where it indicates that the period between the occurrence reported and the time of utterance is relatively short, but the period assessed as short is all before now, that is to say, in past time.) *Soon* is like *then* in Table 6.2, in that it is acceptable with past and future times, but not present: **I'm eating cake soon* is no good if reference is to the present, but is fine with future reference in *I'm catching a train soon*, even though both of these utterances are present progressive in form. In such cases, *soon* is directly anchored to the time of utterance, with the meaning 'a short time after now'. But when *soon* is used with past reference, as in *It began to rain, but soon stopped*, the deixis is indirect, and *soon* means 'a short time after that time'. In the example, 'that time' is the time that the past tense form *began* points to deictically.

2. *Arthur's a tyrant* seems to express a long-lasting situation (a state), and probably represents a judgement about Arthur's personality. *Arthur's being a tyrant* is a longer form, which encourages a pragmatic line of reasoning: why did the speaker not use the shorter alternative? In this case, the use of *being* seems to convey some kind of "provisionality" and invites the inference that, although Arthur is presently being a tyrant, the speaker does not consider 'being a tyrant' to be a general, non-time-specific facet of Arthur's personality.

3. The verb *told* is past simple; *had saved* is past perfect; *were dying* is past progressive.

before time of report	
	time of report
The Gov. saves \$\$\$ ↑	
The co. told the Gov. ... ↑	
People die early.	

The report does not allow certainty over how far the duration of "early dying" should extend to the right: as far as the claim is concerned, it could be that people were still dying early at the time of the report, or the deaths had stopped before the company told the government about it, or that the deaths stopped sometime between the telling and the report. That is, we cannot tell whether the company told the government that "people are dying early", or "people were dying early", or "people have been dying early". It would also be relevant to the diagram to know whether the company told the government "you have saved a lot of money" or "you saved a lot of money". These two possibilities can both be reported by means of a past perfect.

4. *You said you would . . .* or *You said you were going to . . .* are possibilities for (c). The request on the previous day might have been any of *Will you . . ., Would you . . ., Can you . . .* or *Could you . . ..* It would be unusual to use a form such as *You are going to. . .*, or anything along the lines of example (a), because this suggests a high degree of certainty and determination, which would not be appropriate for the asking of a favour from a friend.

Chapter 7

1. As this example hopefully makes clear, the default description without a modal verb is stronger. It is appropriate to use a modal when the speaker lacks direct information about a state of affairs but is presenting a conclusion based on reasoning about the available evidence. Therefore, the presence of modal marking generally invites the inference that the speaker is not really sufficiently sure of the facts to make a non-modal utterance. Of the modal options, *must* indicates more confidence than *might*, but still not as much confidence as would be indicated by the complete omission of the modal marking.

2. *They must be made from buckwheat* can be either deontic (a demand or strong recommendation that buckwheat be used) or epistemic (an inference, perhaps from the colour or taste of the item, that buckwheat is an ingredient).
   We must get up early tomorrow is deontic, and specifies something that, in the speaker's view, needs to be the case. We could imagine it being epistemic in a fictional setting in which the speaker has access to information about what will happen the next day – or indeed a situation in which the speaker is acting as though they have such information, for example in response to a fortune teller predicting

that "Tomorrow you will go on a long journey". Otherwise, what will happen tomorrow is too uncertain to justify epistemic *must.*

The email needn't have been sent can bear either interpretation. On the deontic interpretation it conveys that there was no necessity for the sending of the email; on the epistemic interpretation it conveys that it is possible that the email has not yet been sent. For the author, the former interpretation is preferable (and the latter would be better achieved by . . . *might/may not* . . .).

I can hear you now is a slightly unusual case, in that it indicates "capability": sounds level, transmission and reception conditions mean that what is coming from you is now being heard. Some semanticists take this sort of modality to be similar to deontic: physics and physiology are permitting something to happen. Others would classify this as dynamic modality (mentioned in Section 7.1.3 and treated here as a species of epistemic modality). A pointer to this example being an unusual case is that the modal can be removed without having any substantial effect on the meaning: *I hear you now* is almost a paraphrase of *I can hear you now.*

In *They might or might not make it*, it is somewhat implausible to think of *might* as encoding deontic modality, perhaps because it is hard to imagine permission being given for people to succeed or not succeed. A more natural interpretation of the sentence involves *might* encoding epistemic modality. Although it is generally possible to use *might* to report permission having been given, Biber et al. (1999: 491) found that almost all the usages of *might* in their large sample of conversational and academic English were epistemic.

You better apologise is deontic. This is a reduced form of *You had better apologise* (or *You'd better* . . .). The idiom *had better* is not used to express epistemic modality (see Huddleston and Pullum 2002: 196). We label this an idiom in part because, despite containing the form *had*, it is not used to talk about the past.

3. Many right answers are possible here. For instance:

Guests may check in between 3pm and midnight is epistemic if someone at a hotel is explaining to a new member of staff on the front desk when they should expect people to come to check in. It is deontic if it is the text on a notice showing the permitted checking-in hours.

You must be a musician would be epistemic if said by a taxi driver to a passenger carrying a cello case. If it were spoken by a music teacher to a promising pupil, it could be taken as deontic.

He might say something would be epistemic if it concerns speculation about whether a shy individual at a party will eventually overcome that shyness and join a conversation. It would be deontic if it constituted a complaint that that individual was bringing the mood down by his silence and ought to speak, out of politeness.

4. Deontic *may not* is similar to *can't*: negation has wider scope, giving rise to the meaning 'not (possibly (they have an invitation))'. However, epistemic *may not* behaves like *mustn't*: modality has wider scope, giving rise to the meaning 'possibly (not (they have an invitation))'. For the comparison of relative scope, it does not matter that *may* is represented as 'possibly', using the same word as was used for *can* elsewhere, because the meanings of *may* and *can* share the notion of possibility, the 'negative ruled out' part of their core meanings in Table 7.1.

5. In the situation described, *The witness may | not be named* is deontic, with relative scope 'possibly (not (the witness be named))'. This is different from the general pattern for *may* (as in the preceding question), where there is wider scope for negation when the interpretation is deontic, and wider scope for modality with epistemic interpretations.

6. Based on the "isomorphism" idea, we might expect *one* to have wider scope because it is in the subject noun phrase. On this reading, the sentence describes a single versatile machine that no product escapes being tested by: 'there is one machine (as for every product (the machine tests it))'. However, in this case, there is an opposing tendency for *each* to have wider scope, which makes an alternative reading possible: 'as for every product (there is one machine (the machine tests that product))'. On this reading, we are still assured that every product is tested by a machine, but it could be a different machine for each different type of product.

Chapter 8

1. In this example, B probably succeeds in communicating their identity to A, because A can infer this from hearing their voice. Just in propositional terms, it looks as though the maxim of quantity is being disobeyed, because no new information is supplied. However, this can be seen as reasonable if it is taken as a signal that no additional information is needed because the voice should be immediately recognisable. If this is the case, then this minimal utterance is adequate for the communicative purpose, and a more explicit utterance – such as B giving their name – would arguably violate the maxim of quantity (by providing more information than needed) or manner (by being more verbose than necessary).

2. The continuation *and that's all there is to it* seems to evoke the quantity maxim: it conveys that nothing more can be said on the subject that

is relevant to the communicative needs of the situation. The framing *Let me make this clear* evokes the maxim of manner, and suggests that formulation is maximally straightforward and perhaps that it holds no hidden meanings.

3. Assuming that B is cooperative, the failure to answer A's question directly could be taken to implicate that B doesn't know the answer to A's question. The content of the proposition that B actually expresses could also be taken to implicate that the sociolinguistics books aren't (also) at the end of the shelf – the utterance suggests that B is knowledgeable about the books at the end of the shelf and that the psycholinguistics books aren't among them.

4. Taken literally, *I could not fail to disagree with you less* affirms that 'I couldn't disagree with you more' – that is to say, 'I disagree with you'. The original formulation blatantly violates the manner implicature. In this case, it's not very clear what the speaker actually intends to convey, although possibilities include a command of deceptive language or an unwillingness to give a direct answer.

5. The utterance conveys that *it* was a fluid and entered the basement slowly. The latter meaning is an entailment because it cannot be cancelled without contradiction: it would be odd to say **It seeped into the basement in a sudden rush*. Moreover, the inference that it entered the basement slowly only arises from the positive form of the sentence, and wouldn't arise from its negative counterpart *It didn't seep into the basement*. The inference that *it* was a fluid is a presupposition: it is conveyed by both the positive sentence that was uttered and its negative counterpart, but in the latter case it is cancellable without contradiction: *It didn't seep into the basement; wet rot is a fungus*.

6. There are various possible answers. One class of situation in which it seems to be acceptable to say something like these sentences is when the presupposition has already been introduced by someone else. For instance, if someone affirms that *Jessica regretted arguing with her boss*, but you know that they are actually thinking of someone else (say, *Jane*), it seems to be OK to respond *Jessica didn't regret arguing with her boss* before continuing *You're thinking of Jane*. It would be clear that you weren't committed to the truth of Jessica having argued with her boss, even though you had uttered a sentence that formally presupposed it. Similar contexts of utterance would rescue the other two example sentences as well.

Chapter 9

1. This is an example of metonymy: *beaks* is used as a metonym for *birds*. This is supported both by the knowledge that birds have beaks, and that the corresponding metonymy *mouths* is used for human dependents.

2. *He's a tube light* was intended to convey that the person in question was slow on the uptake, similarly to how a fluorescent light reacts slowly to the operation of the switch. The background information that is relevant to this interpretation is that the salient feature of fluorescent lights (available in Fiji at the time) was that they were slow to light up and generally rather dim.

3. Based on the occurrences of *like*, it initially appears that Ali's remark involves two similes. However, given that bees actually do sting, *sting like a bee* is in itself literal rather than figurative – and, on a charitably broad interpretation of *float*, the same could be said of *float like a butterfly*. But Ali himself is the understood subject of both clauses – he could equivalently have said *I float like a butterfly, I sting like a bee* – and in that respect both of the clauses are in fact metaphorical, because Ali himself did not literally float or literally sting.

4. In principle, the comparison between Andy Murray and a weekend in Worthing could be said to be literal: although this involves comparing entities from two dissimilar semantic categories, it involves comparing them on a scale on which such dissimilar entities can nevertheless be judged (the scale of "dullness"). However, the end of Murray's remark is probably intended to be ironic. Whether or not he means to convey that the criticism is unfair, it seems unlikely that he should be more concerned about the feelings of a seaside town than about his own feelings: particularly given that all that was literally said about Worthing was that a weekend there is more interesting than Andy Murray, which wouldn't be grounds to take offence.

   Alternatively, there is an interpretation available in which Murray's remark, although intended as a joke, is nevertheless intended to be literally true. It's possible that he is conveying the idea that it is unfair on Worthing to use it as a benchmark for dullness. This would be particularly applicable if he interpreted the initial criticism as an exaggeration – that is, that the author of the original quote overstated his dullness rhetorically by comparing him unfavourably to the dullest thing they could imagine. On this interpretation, the initial criticism of Worthing can be interpreted as more damning than the criticism of Murray himself, and grounds for objection. Cases such as this admit various different interpretations in terms of figures of speech, and it is often unclear which analysis is most appropriate without asking the speaker(s).

Chapter 10

1. It is a reasonable assumption about prototypical hearers that each has a head, which justifies immediate use of definite reference. And the warning about the step would typically be given in a situation in which it is possible for the addressee to experience the step directly, for example by looking or by tapping it with a stick, again making it part of the background without further ado. The answer is not simply that warnings of this kind have to be issued in a hurry, as there is no barrier to using indefinites in such cases, for instance where the danger is not so accessible: *Careful, there's a snake in there.*

2. Between these two versions of the pseudo-cleft, the presuppositions are the same, namely (in this case) that 'something hit the sofa'. This is still what is conveyed by the negated versions of both forms of the sentence: *It wasn't the meteorite that hit the sofa* and *What hit the sofa wasn't the meteorite.*

3. It would be reasonable to correct Tom by saying either "No, you're wrong: Lucy borrowed the DICtionary", or "No, you're wrong: it was the DICtionary that Lucy borrowed". Both of these relate to scenario (b) in which Lucy borrowed something, although it wasn't the atlas. This is because Tom's *it*-cleft presupposes that 'Lucy borrowed something', and that presupposition is satisfied by the information in (b) rather than that in (a).

4. It seems that these kinds of usage are acceptable if the Question Under Discussion in some sense involves the presuppositional expression. For instance, if the QUD is "whether Jessica regretted arguing with her boss", it is reasonable to respond *Jessica didn't regret arguing with her boss* before explaining the presupposition failure (*You're thinking of Jane*). The specific case discussed in an earlier exercise, in which the preceding turn involves someone erroneously asserting that *Jessica regretted arguing with her boss*, is a special case of this, because that sentence could also be interpreted as answering the QUD of "whether Jessica regretted arguing with her boss".

Chapter 11

1. The speech act of warning bus riders not to smoke (or perhaps threatening them with adverse consequences) is mitigated by presenting part of it as a speech act of thanking. Thanking presupposes

that the addressee has done something that is appreciated by the bus company. The mitigation is perhaps addressed to habitually non-smoking passengers, who might otherwise have been affronted by the apparent presumption that they needed to be warned not to smoke.

2. (a) Literally a question, this has the force of an order.
   (b) Literally an order, this has the force of an offer.
   (c) Literally a question, this has the force of a statement.
   (d) Literally a statement, this has the force of an expression of sympathy or condolence.
   (e) Literally an order, this has the force of a statement.
   (f) Literally an order, this has the force of an expression of condolence.
   (g) Literally a question, this has the force of a statement (to the effect of 'I have never let you down') – it is what is called a "rhetorical question".
   (h) Literally a statement, this has the force of a recommendation.

3. "I should let you go" appears to serve primarily as a device for bringing about the end of a conversation. Formally, it makes a deontic statement about what the speaker should permit to happen. By articulating this, the speaker could be said to implicitly give this permission. However, giving this permission further suggests that the recipient might wish to avail themselves of this permission. By calling attention to the fact that the hearer may leave the conversation, the speaker invites the inference that the speaker thinks the hearer should leave the conversation, and hence that the conversation should come to an end. Compared with "I should go", the form "I should let you go" is arguably more polite, in that it suggests that the pressing calls on the hearer's time (rather than on the speaker's time) are the reason that the conversation should end. However, to the extent that it has become euphemistic for "I wish to end this conversation", that effect of additional politeness is arguably being eroded by custom.

References

Austin, J. L. (1962), *How to Do Things with Words*, Oxford: Oxford University Press.

Biber, Douglas, Stig Johansson, Geoffrey Leech, Susan Conrad and Edward Finegan (1999), *Longman Grammar of Spoken and Written English*, Harlow: Pearson.

Cann, Ronnie (1993), *Formal Semantics*, Cambridge: Cambridge University Press.

Carston, Robyn (2010), 'XIII – Metaphor: ad hoc concepts, literal meaning and mental images', *Proceedings of the Aristotelian Society* (Hardback), 110: 295–321.

Chomsky, Noam (1981), *Lectures on Government and Binding*, Dordrecht: Foris Publications.

Clark, Herbert H. (2004), 'Pragmatics of language performance', in Laurence R. Horn and Gregory Ward (eds), *Handbook of Pragmatics*, Oxford: Blackwell, pp. 365–82.

Clark, Herbert H. (2012), 'Wordless questions, wordless answers', in J. P. de Ruiter (ed.), *Questions: Formal, Functional and Interactional Perspectives*, Cambridge: Cambridge University Press, pp. 81–100.

Clark, Herbert H. and Richard J. Gerrig (1984), 'On the pretense theory of irony', *Journal of Experimental Psychology: General*, 113: 121–6.

Croft, William (1991), *Syntactic Categories and Grammatical Relations: The Cognitive Organization of Information*, Chicago: University of Chicago Press.

Croft, William and Alan Cruse (2004), *Cognitive Linguistics*, Cambridge: Cambridge University Press.

Cruse, Alan (2011), *Meaning in Language*, 3rd edn, Oxford: Oxford University Press.

De Swart, Henriëtte and Helen de Hoop (2000), 'Topic and focus', in L. Cheng and R. Sybesma (eds), *The First Glot International State-of-the-Article Book*, Berlin: Mouton de Gruyter, pp. 105–30.

Dowty, David (1991), 'Thematic proto-roles and argument selection', *Language*, 67: 547–619.

Elbourne, Paul (2011), *Meaning: A Slim Guide to Semantics*, Oxford: Oxford University Press.

Fellbaum, Christiane (2000), 'Autotroponymy', in Y. Ravin and C. Leacock (eds), *Polysemy: Theoretical and Computational Approaches*, Oxford: Oxford University Press, pp. 52–67.

Feynman, Richard P. (1999), *The Pleasure of Finding Things Out*, New York: Perseus.

Gibbs, Raymond W., Jr. (1994), *The Poetics of Mind: Figurative Thought, Language, and Understanding*, New York: Cambridge University Press.

Giegerich, Heinz J. (1992), *English Phonology: An Introduction*, Cambridge: Cambridge University Press.

Glucksberg, Sam (2008), 'How metaphors create categories – quickly', in R. W. Gibbs, Jr. (ed.), *The Cambridge Handbook of Metaphor and Thought*, Cambridge: Cambridge University Press, pp. 67–83.

Glucksberg, Sam and Boaz Keysar (1990), 'Understanding metaphorical comparisons: beyond similarity', *Psychological Review*, 97: 3–18.

Gordon, David and George Lakoff (1971), 'Conversational postulates', *Papers from the Seventh Regional Meeting of the Chicago Linguistic Society*, Chicago: Chicago Linguistic Society, pp. 63–84.

Grant, Lynn and Laurie Bauer (2004), 'Criteria for re-defining idioms: are we barking up the wrong tree?', *Applied Linguistics*, 25: 38–61.

Grice, H. Paul (1975), 'Logic and conversation', in P. Cole and J. L. Morgan (eds), *Syntax and Semantics*, vol. 3, New York: Academic Press, pp. 41–58.

Grice, H. Paul (1989), *Studies in the Way of Words*, Cambridge, MA: Harvard University Press.

Groefsema, Marjolein (1995), '*Can, may, must* and *should*: a Relevance theoretic account', *Journal of Linguistics*, 31: 53–79.

Grundy, Peter (2000), *Doing Pragmatics*, 2nd edn, London: Edward Arnold.

Hewson, John and Vit Bubenik (1997), *Tense and Aspect in Indo-European Languages*, Amsterdam: John Benjamins.

Horn, Laurence R. (1984), 'Towards a new taxonomy for pragmatic inference: Q-based and R-based implicature', in D. Schiffrin (ed.), *Meaning, Form and Use in Context*, Washington: Georgetown University Press, pp. 11–42.

Horn, Laurence R. (1989), *A Natural History of Negation*, Chicago: University of Chicago Press.

Huang, Yan (2006), *Pragmatics*, Oxford: Oxford University Press.

Huddleston, Rodney and Geoffrey K. Pullum (2002), *The Cambridge Grammar of the English Language*, Cambridge: Cambridge University Press.

Imai, Mutsumi (2000), 'Universal ontological knowledge and a bias toward language-specific categories in the construal of individuation', in S. Niemeyer and R. Dirven (eds), *Evidence for Linguistic Relativity*, Amsterdam: Benjamins, pp. 139–60.

Johannsen, Katrin and J. P. de Ruiter (2013), 'The role of scene type and priming in the processing and selection of a spatial frame of reference', *Frontiers in Psychology*, 4: 182.

Jurafsky, Dan (2004), 'Pragmatics and computational linguistics', in

Laurence R. Horn and Gregory Ward (eds), *Handbook of Pragmatics*, Oxford: Blackwell, pp. 578–604.

Kearns, Kate (2011), *Semantics*, 2nd edn, Basingstoke: Macmillan.

Kennedy, Chris (2012), 'Adjectives', in G. Russell and D. Graff Fara (eds), *The Routledge Companion to Philosophy of Language*, New York: Routledge, pp. 328–41.

Klein, Wolfgang (1992), 'The present perfect puzzle', *Language*, 68: 525–52.

Lappin, Shalom (2001), 'An introduction to formal semantics', in M. Aronoff and J. Rees-Miller (eds), *The Handbook of Linguistics*, Oxford: Blackwell, pp. 369–93.

Leech, Geoffrey (1983), *Principles of Pragmatics*, London: Longman.

Leech, Geoffrey, Paul Rayson and Andrew Wilson (2001), *Word Frequencies in Spoken and Written English*, Harlow: Pearson Education.

Levinson, Stephen C. (1983), *Pragmatics*, Cambridge: Cambridge University Press.

Levinson, Stephen C. (2000), *Presumptive Meanings: The Theory of Generalized Conversational Implicature*, Cambridge, MA: MIT Press.

Lycan, William G. (2000), *Philosophy of Language*, London: Routledge.

Lyons, John (1977), *Semantics*, Cambridge: Cambridge University Press.

McNally, Louise (2011), 'The relative role of property type and scale structure in explaining the behavior of gradable adjectives', in R. Nouwen, R. van Rooij, U. Sauerland and H.-C. Schmitz (eds), *VIC 2009: Papers from the ESSLLI 2009 Workshop on Vagueness in Communication* (Lecture Notes in Artificial Intelligence 6517), Berlin: Springer, pp. 151–68.

Mervis, Carolyn B. and Eleanor Rosch (1981), 'Categorization of natural objects', *Annual Review of Psychology*, 32: 89–115.

Miller, George A. and Christiane Fellbaum (1991), 'Semantic networks of English', *Cognition*, 41: 197–229.

Miller, Jim (2002), *An Introduction to English Syntax*, Edinburgh: Edinburgh University Press.

Musolino, Julien, Stephen Crain and Rosalind Thornton (2000), 'Navigating negative quantification space', *Linguistics*, 38: 1–32.

Palmer, Frank (1990), *Modality and the English Modals*, 3rd edn, London: Longman.

Papafragou, Anna (2000), *Modality: Issues in the Semantics–Pragmatics Interface*, Amsterdam: Elsevier.

Perrault, C. Raymond and James F. Allen (1980), 'A plan-based analysis of indirect speech acts', *Computational Linguistics*, 6: 167–82.

Quirk, Randolph, Sidney Greenbaum, Jan Svartvik and Geoffrey Leech (1985), *A Comprehensive Grammar of the English Language*, London: Longman.

Radford, Andrew (2004), *Minimalist Syntax*, Cambridge: Cambridge University Press.

Roberts, Craige (2012), 'Information structure: towards an integrated formal theory of pragmatics', *Semantics and Pragmatics*, 5 (6): 1–69.

Rooth, Mats (1996), 'Focus', in S. Lappin (ed.), *The Handbook of Contemporary Semantic Theory*, Oxford: Blackwell, pp. 271–97.

Saeed, John I. (2015), *Semantics*, 4th edn, Oxford: Blackwell.

Schegloff, Emanuel A. and Harvey Sacks (1973), 'Opening up closings', *Semiotica*, VIII (4): 289–327.

Searle, John R. (1975), 'Indirect speech acts', in P. Cole and J. L. Morgan (eds), *Syntax and Semantics*, vol. 3, New York: Academic Press, pp. 59–82.

Searle, John R. (1979), *Expression and Meaning: Studies in the Theory of Speech Acts*, Cambridge: Cambridge University Press.

Solt, Stephanie (2011), 'How many mosts?', in I. Reich, E. Horch and D. Pauly (eds), *Proceedings of Sinn und Bedeutung 15*, Saarbrücken: Universaar, pp. 565–79.

Sperber, Dan and Deirdre Wilson (1981), 'On verbal irony', in P. Cole (ed.), *Radical Pragmatics*, New York: Academic Press, pp. 295–318.

Sperber, Dan and Deirdre Wilson (1995), *Relevance: Communication and Cognition*, 2nd edn, Oxford: Blackwell.

Stern, Josef (2000), *Metaphor in Context*, Cambridge, MA: MIT Press.

Tenny, Carol (2000), 'Core events and adverbial modification', in C. Tenny and J. Pustejovsky (eds), *Events as Grammatical Objects: The Converging Perspectives of Lexical Semantics and Syntax*, Stanford, CA: CSLI, pp. 285–334.

Trask, R. L. (1993), *A Dictionary of Grammatical Terms in Linguistics*, London: Routledge.

Traugott, Elizabeth Closs (2000), 'Semantic change: an overview', in L. Cheng and R. Sybesma (eds), *The First Glot International State-of-the-Article Book*, Berlin: Mouton de Gruyter, pp. 385–406.

Van der Auwera, Johan and Vladimir A. Plungian (1998), 'Modality's semantic map', *Linguistic Typology*, 2: 79–124.

Vendler, Zeno (1957), 'Verbs and times', *The Philosophical Review*, 66: 143–60.

Wilson, Deirdre (2006), 'The pragmatics of verbal irony: echo or pretence?', *Lingua*, 116: 1722–43.

Wilson, Deirdre and Dan Sperber (2002), 'Relevance theory', *UCL Working Papers in Linguistics*, 14: 249–90.

Wittgenstein, Ludwig (1953), *Philosophical Investigations*, Oxford: Blackwell.

Index

Note: Bold print page numbers indicate where some aspect of a technical term is explained. Closely related forms are listed together. The exercises and suggested answers are referenced only where they add significantly to what is in the main text.